S0-EGR-232

@Copyright 2019by Dorothy Grin- **All rights reserved.**

This document is geared towards providing exact and reliable information in regards to the topic and issue covered. The publication is sold with the idea that the publisher is not required to render accounting, officially permitted, or otherwise, qualified services. If advice is necessary, legal or professional, a practiced individual in the profession should be ordered.

Under no circumstance will any legal responsibility or blame be held against the publisher for any reparation, damages, or monetary loss due to the information herein, either directly or indirectly.

Legal Notice: The book is copyright protected. This is only for personal use. You cannot amend, distribute, sell, use, quote or paraphrase any part or the content within this book without the consent of the author.

Disclaimer Notice: Please note the information contained within this document is for educational and entertainment purposes only. Every attempt has been made to provide accurate, up to date and reliable complete information. No warranties of any kind are expressed or implied. Readers acknowledge that the author is not engaging in the rendering of legal, financial, medical or professional advice. The content of this book has been derived from various sources. Please consult a licensed professional before attempting any techniques outlined in this book.

CONTENTS

Chapter 1: Basic Overview

Roller Turner discovered in 1921 that ketone bodies like acetoacetate, acetone, and β-hydroxybutyrate were created by the liver if you engage in an eating routine involving low carbs and high fats. He discovered this pioneering information while examining the link among dietary regimen, diabetes, and their correlations. Dr. Russel Wilder further assessed these discoveries and presented the world with the ketogenic diet, which was then utilized on patients with epilepsy in 1921 to check the impact of diet on them, and the astonishing outcomes. The Keto diet includes explicitly plant-based nourishments, rich in carbs and can as a vitality hotspot for the successful and reliable body's functioning. The eating regimen delivers various medical advantages, which incorporate upgraded productivity of the body, solid digestion, and weight reduction.

What does "Keto" signify?

The body begins utilizing ketones, rather than glucose, as a vitality mechanism for its working on the ketogenic diet. The ketones are mindful, or the word 'keto' in the eating regimen plan is used in the base nearness of glucose in the body. Ketones are delivered by eating a low carb diet and a moderate protein supply. The primary creation of ketones is fats; in turn, they are produced in the liver. They are utilized for the working of the body, including the cerebrum.

Modification to ketones from glucose results in over the top fat consumption while it also reduces insulin levels in the body. This has a rash impact on getting thinner separated from different other medical advantages. The effective strategy to create ketones is extremely quick. In any case, as fasting isn't possible due to its prolonged time, the keto diet is an elective way to deal with fasting, so it offers similar advantages to fasting without actually fasting by any stretch of the imagination.

Who Shouldn't Try the Ketogenic Diet?

As a rule, the keto diet is quite rigid, so individuals who fall under the accompanying classes must seek advice from their specialists before trying this eating routine. Patients with these issues include:

- Diabetic Patients
- Blood Pressure related Patients
- Breastfeeding Mothers

Guidance for Breastfeeding Mothers and Diabetics

It is risky to eat a strict low-carb diet while breastfeeding, so a more secure low-carb diet is advised that includes 50g carbs/day. You can accomplish this goal by adding 3-4 substantial organic products to your strict routine. If you experience any adverse signs, quickly visit a specialist. It is likewise recommended to drink an adequate supply of water to reduce the danger of drying out for milk creation. Improve your fiber, fats and veggie consumption for keeping up your vitality levels. For breastfeeding, consider a somewhat reasonable keto plan rather than a severe one.

Generally, the Keto diet is not suggested for diabetics to ensure a stringent eating routine, but carefully check your glucose levels on a regular schedule to maintain them. Diabetics must additionally keep a mind a goal to ensure stable ketone levels in their bodies to stay away from the danger of DKA (Diabetic Ketoacidosis) or in exceptional cases unconsciousness. It's prescribed by the ADA (American Diabetes Association) to test your ketones if your glucose outperforms 240mg/dL.

What Are the Signs of Ketosis?

There are numerous indicators to realize that you are in ketosis, which incorporates breath, blood, and/or urine testing. Notwithstanding these tests, there are physical side effects of ketosis which don't require any analysis whatsoever. They are as follows:

1.   **Increment Thirst and Dry Mouth:**

There is plausibility of having a dry mouth if you aren't sufficiently absorbing electrolytes like salt and/or drinking enough water. It is prescribed to drink as much water as could reasonably expected by sufficiently swallowing bouillon; for example, 1-2 containers every day. There will be a specific metallic preference in your body.

2.   **An increment in Urination:**

A ketonic compound called 'acetoacetate' might excrete in urine. This feature makes it simple to test ketosis by utilizing pee strips. In the underlying stages, it additionally results in successive pee. It is the primary purpose behind the expansion in thirst (clarified previously).

3.   **Keto breath:**

The particular breath called the 'keto breath' is because of a compound called acetone.. It causes the breath to exude a specific 'fruity' smell or a smell like that of nail paint remover. You can likewise detect this particular smell in the wake of perspiring while at the same time completing any exercise. This condition is brief and diminishes with time.

4.   **An increment in Energy:**

After going through the 'keto influenza,' which results in tiredness, individuals often experience a specific increase in vitality levels. It can likewise manifest in expanded concentration and focus or even in a feeling of elation.

5.   **The decrease in Hunger:**

This outcome can be credited to the body's use of the surplus vitality from storage of fats. Individuals feel happy with just a couple of eating regimens daily, bringing about intermittent fasting unwittingly, sparing both cash and time by speeding one's weight reduction.

Chapter 2: What Are the Benefits of the Keto Diet?

The upsides of the keto diet are highly weight control plans dependent on low carb consumption; the main contrast is that the keto diet is the more dominant and productive in its advantages. In essence, the keto diet is a low carb diet plan with super-charged forces contrasted with its rivals and offers the most visible benefits for users. A couple of its impressive merits are noted:

1.   Weight reduction:

The way in which the body utilizes fat as a vitality source clearly reiterates how the keto diet is advantageous in weight reduction. Fat misfortune is invigorated as the insulin levels decline. This circumstance gives a perfect catalyst for extreme fat loss, fostering weight reduction successfully without much appetite. Studies from over 20 present-day papers have confirmed that the Keto diet is more successful than other comparative eating regimen designed for weight reduction factors.

2.   Controlled Appetite:

The Keto diet gives you a chance to control your craving. This regulation is because when fats are scorched definitely, the body approaches surplus vitality from them and decreases one's appetite. This control of craving likewise results in progressively successful weight reduction. It similarly facilitates the intermittent fasting and generates the inversion of type 2 diabetes from invigorating weight reduction. It is additionally entirely practical monetarily, as it diminishes your use on grocery bills and sustenance due to decreased appetite.

The lower desire to eat nourishment or control hunger both additionally cause a strategic distance from sugar and sustenance fixation from dietary issues like bulimia and so on. The sentiment of fulfillment is a fundamental piece of the arrangement. Nourishment turns into a companion and an energizing source, rather than an adversary, with the Ketogenic diet plan.

3. Surplus Energy and Mental Boosting:

The procedure of ketosis gives a consistent stream of vitality as ketones to the cerebrum help to maintain a strategic distance from glucose swings. This outcome offers progress in mental concentration and focus; furthermore, it also cleans up cerebrum haze as well. The fundamental explanation behind the prominence of the Keto diet is its benefits concerning emotional well-being and core interest. These advantages can be effectively experienced while in ketosis. Amid ketosis, the human mind is furnished with surplus vitality nonstop with ketones, not carbs, which is the purpose behind the improved mental execution of the human body.

4. Turning around Type-2 Diabetes and Controlling Blood Sugar:

It is further credited for reducing glucose levels in the body and decreasing the negative job of higher insulin levels. The idea that the keto diet is effective in turning around type 2 diabetes likewise reiterates that it is instrumental for transforming pre-diabetic conditions.

5. Improvement in Health Markers:

Lower carb consumption results in progress for essentially wellbeing markers like glucose levels, cholesterol levels (triglycerides and HDL) and circulatory strain. These wellbeing markers are related to metabolic disorders, weight gains, upgrades, inversion of type 2 diabetes, and belly fat, etc.

6. Stomach Improvement:

The Keto diet has numerous compelling upgrades in stomach wellbeing. It brings down issues and agonies by lowering gas in the stomach. It may be experienced within u 2-3 days of following the ketogenic diet plan. FODMAP contains a high measure of carbs, and they begin maturation in the small digestive tract. which prompts swelling and gas. The gut dividers are unfit to assimilate them legitimately and cause the liquid to stick in the digestive tract along these lines, which fosters a looseness of the bowels. The Keto diet is a much lower FODMAP diet and serves as an enemy of the IBS approach. The moderate expulsion of carbs from your eating regimen improves your stomach related framework immensely.

7.   Improvement in Physical Strength:

The Keto diet improves physical quality and continuance a great deal because of the arrangement of a conventional and steady supply of vitality from fats. Energy due to carbs (glycogen) in the body just for a couple of long periods of abnormal state working out, as opposed to this the energy from fat sources goes on for a considerable length of time or even a very long time in the body and upgrades the physical exhibitions of the collection.

8.   Epilepsy Treatment:

The Keto diet has been beneficial for the treatment of epilepsy since the 1920s. it was formerly utilized for kids; however, at this point it has likewise been connected to grown-ups and has assisted them. With the Ketogenic diet, patients of epilepsy either take less or no medicine for their treatment, without the dread of any seizures. This likewise reduces the reactions of medications by decreasing medication admission and assumes a great role in psychological well-being improvement.

Chapter 3: How to Accomplish 'Ketosis'

Numerous variables assume a primary job in improving and expanding the ketosis levels. They are recorded underneath in their significance from high to low:

1.   Limitation of carbs:

Decreasing carb admission to simply an edible 20grams/day or lower is deemed as a carefully low carb diet and can improve the ketosis levels a great deal. Understand that fiber admission doesn't need to be brought down as it is a helpful supplement. It is essential to note that exclusively reducing carb utilization can result in ketosis, and the remainder of each measure taken for ketosis improvement guarantees the accomplishment of ketosis.

2.   Limitation of Proteins:

Limiting protein admission to a direct dimension essential in the Ketogenic diet plan. Surplus utilization of proteins will result in their transformation into glucose, hence lowering the ketosis levels. The most ordinarily dedicated oversight by Keto devotees is higher utilization of proteins which ought to be decreased to direct use as it were. The perfect measure of protein admission ought to be 1g/kg the heaviness of the body for example around 80g of protein if you are 80kgs.

3.   Devour Enough Fat:

There is a contrast between fasting and the Keto diet for ketosis. The Ketogenic diet plan can be followed in a steady way while persistent fasting is challenging to accomplish and fairly destructive to the body. The adverse effects of starving include craving, tiredness and surrendering; while the ketogenic diet can be effectively connected to day by day lives and pursued without any obstacle and delivers plenty of advantages. Eating enough fat is imperative: and if you are feeling hungrier constantly, strive at adding more fat to your dinners like progressively adding olive oil and so on.

4.   Have a go at abstaining from nibbling:

It is recommended not to have a meal if you are not feeling hungry enough. Eating over your requirements negatively affects ketosis, and it moderates the procedure of ketosis close by abating weight reduction as well. You can decide on a ketogenic snack if you feel a certain yearning.

5.   Irregular Fasting:

Rather than complete fasting, intermittent fasting helps a great deal in ketosis. The best intermittent fasting is eating just for 8 hours in the day and fasting amid the remaining of the 16 hours. It is compelling for raising ketone levels, inversion of type 2 diabetes, and stimulating weight reduction.

6.   Normal Exercising:

Practicing lower carb utilization drastically fosters the procedure of ketosis. Moreover, it additionally improves weight reduction procedure and inversion of type 2 diabetes subtly. Practicing isn't fundamental to accomplish ketosis; instead, it helps with improving ketosis.

7.   Adequate Sleep:

The standard of having enough rest is considered a normal of 7-8 hours every night. It is prescribed to get appropriate rest time and keep your feelings of anxiety lower. Stress hormones and lack of sleep risk raising glucose levels, bringing down ketosis levels, and marginally impacts in backing off weight reduction as well. It likewise makes it difficult to pursue the Keto diet plan and keep away from enticements for eating in opposition to the arrangement. Sound rest and lower feelings of anxiety do not lead to ketosis instead help in improving the procedure.

Indisputably, to accomplish ketosis, bring down the carb admission to very low dimensions. It is ideal to lower them to roughly 20 carbs every day. IT is the most fundamental factor for accomplishing ketosis. For improving ketosis levels, begin embracing the previously mentioned variables from start to finish.

Chapter 4: Foods for Keto Diet

Foods which are prescribed:

The accompanying foods are viewed as the best for the Keto lover diet plan. They are impressively low in carbs. These include:

- Above ground veggies like cauliflower, broccoli, and zucchini and so forth.
- Leafy green vegetables such as spinach, kale, and so forth.
- Seeds and nuts ranging from almonds, pumpkin seeds, sunflower seeds, and pistachios and so forth.
- Berries like blackberries, raspberries, and other effect berries, which are low glycemic in nature.
- Avocados
- Sweeteners such as Erythritol, Stevia, and different sugars, which are low carb in nature.
- Fats like MCT oil, coconut oil, red palm oil, and so forth.

Foods which are not prescribed:

The accompanying classifications of food are not permitted while following the keto lover diet plan. These examples are high in their carb contents and can negatively hinder your plan:

- Legumes like peas, lentils, and dark beans and so on.
- Grains such as grains, rice, wheat, and corn and so on.
- Sugar-rich sustenance like maple syrup, agave, and nectar and so on.
- Tubers including yams, and potatoes and so forth.
- Fruits like oranges, bananas, and apples, etc.

Protein Carb Ratio:

Your sustenance on the keto lover plan should be high in fat substance and somewhat high in protein as protein for the most part since protein is convertible in the body to body sugar. An unpleasant sketch recommends that roughly 5% vitality ought to be from carbs (bring down the number of carbs, the more the adequacy). 15-25% should be from protein and practically 75% should derive from fat.

How to Consume More Fat?

The fundamental purpose of fats in the keto diet comes from high-fat dairy and eggs. They are numerous extra fat sources, too, which can be used on the keto diet. These incorporate different plant-based oils, which can be utilized as an option in contrast to the creature fats commonly used for preparing and cooking purposes. A portion of these fat sources embody the following:

- Coconut Oil
- MCT Oil
- Avocado Oil
- Olive Oil
- Red Palm Oil

What is Suggested for Drinking?

Water is viewed as the most prescribed and ideal refreshment for Keto sweethearts. Notwithstanding water, espresso and tea can likewise be devoured, yet it is vital to remembered that you don't need to utilize any sugars or sugar substitutes. A little amount of milk or cream in espresso or tea is satisfactory, yet not an espresso latte. The periodic utilization of a single glass of wine is additionally permitted.

Chapter 5: General Mistakes by Beginners

The Keto diet can be very confusing to beginners, and they might unintentionally be committing mistakes which will hinder the effectiveness of the diet plan. Some of the common errors are as follows:

1. **Obsession with Weight Scale:**
Everyone's body reacts differently to the keto diet; some may lose weight instantly, while others might take some time in achieving weight loss. Above all the Keto diet isn't only about weight, so don't have an obsession of merely assessing the weight scale.

2. **Consuming Processed Fats:**
Seed and vegetable oils are mostly processed fats and are a health danger. They cause conditions like cancer, increased cholesterol levels, and even heart attacks.

3. **Not consuming Adequate Fats:**
It is tough to maintain your fat intake while being new to Keto. Maintain a proper intake of fats to make the plan work.

4. **Avoiding Meal Planning:**
Meal planning is essential for a Keto diet. If you don't plan, you will eventually lose access to the required macros and end up eating food which might knock you out of your ketosis. Plan effectively to follow this diet.

5. **Excessive Protein Intake:**
Proteins in Keto are used to maintain the muscle mass, and fats are used as the energy source only. Excessive protein intake can result in increasing glucose levels which will affect your ketosis. Planning your diet can maintain your protein intake as required.

6. **Keto Isn't a Quick Fix:**
Keto isn't just a diet, it's a complete lifestyle! Following it for a short time and then leaving the plan will lead you to exactly where you started it. If you are looking for a quick fix for your weight, just cut off sugar from your diet, but Keto is a lifetime approach to adapt.

7.   Stop Comparing:

Keto might react differently on different people. Everyone has a unique body effect on the diet, stop comparing your results with others. Instead, focus on following your diet strictly to achieve your results and live a healthy lifestyle.

8.   Stay Hydrated:

Drinking adequate water intake is extremely necessary for Keto followers. You might be losing water from sweating, so drink enough to remain hydrated.

Chapter 6: Baking

Baking and Its Advantages:

There are various reasons why you should make your own baked items. We are going to explain the prominent reasons which will compel you to start baking at your home. These reasons are essential:

1.   It is a healthier approach:

If you carefully observe the ingredient labels on baked items that you buy in the stores, you are going to find out that there are various chemicals and other preservatives that are used to keep them fresh. These chemicals have many adverse effects on your health in the longer run. You can add various other ingredients to add flavor like herbs, dry fruits, etc. All these ingredients must comply with the Keto foods, as allowed in the diet plan:

2.   Offers more taste:

Baked items, like a loaf of homemade bread, offer more flavor and nutrition than the ones that are available in the markets. The logical reason to understand is that the baked items are fresh, have healthy ingredients, and of course, you are the master of them. Add whatever suits your taste, and you can have a variety of baked items with just a little effort.

3.   Financially beneficial:

Apart from the healthy benefits homemade baked items offers, you are going to save a lot of money for yourself and also gain a nutritious lifestyle. You can avoid various medical complications and save medical care expenses, also. Instead of buying bread from the market, you can make your own with a minimal amount of money.

4.   Weight loss:

The Keto diet is beneficial in giving you a drastic weight loss while maintaining the nutrients and overall health of your body. The Keto baked items will ensure that you have all the necessary nutrients in your meal plan. Yet, you are going to have a smooth weight loss process without the fear of getting knocked out of it. The Keto baked items offer much lesser carbs than the regular items and keep your blood glucose levels under control.

FAQs regarding Keto Baked items:

1.   What is Keto bread?

Keto bread is basically a combination of coconut flour or almond flour, xanthan gum, eggs, and healthy fats. Generally, it looks similar to regular wheat bread but offers 20 percent lower carbs than the regular wheat bread.

2.   Can we make our Keto baked items dairy-free?

You can make your Keto baked items dairy-free by simply putting ½ cup of olive oil as an alternative to butter.

3.   What is the best alternative to xanthan gum while making Keto baked items?

The primary purpose of xanthan gum is that it is a thickening agent, but in case of a Keto baked item, it is used for slicing them by acting as a binding agent. The following alternatives work the best if you don't have xanthan gum:

- Guar gum (1 tbsp)
- Gelatin Powder (1 tbsp)
- Ground Chia Seeds (1 tbsp)

4.   Can coconut flour be used as an alternative to almond flour?

You can use coconut flour as an alternative to almond flour by maintaining a ratio of ½ cups of coconut flour to 2 cups of almond flour. This ratio is because the coconut flour has more absorbing quality than almond flour.

5.   What is the best way to store keto baked items?

You can first slice the baked items, and then you can then store these pieces into two different containers; one in the freezer for using it next week while the other one in the fridge for the week going on.

6.   How many carbs are there in the keto bread?

The Keto bread offers a significant 20 percent lesser carbs than the regular wheat bread.

Chapter 7: Bread Baking for Beginners Recipes

• Keto Bread

Serves: 6
Prep Time: 5 hours 10 mins
This delicious low-carb and Keto bread couldn't be any easier to make!

Ingredients
- 6 large eggs, separated
- ¼ teaspoon cream of tartar
- 6 drops liquid stevia
- 1½ cups almond flour
- ¼ cup butter, melted
- 3 teaspoons baking powder
- 1 pinch pink salt

Directions
1. Preheat oven to 365 degrees F and grease a loaf pan.
2. Whisk together egg whites with cream of tartar.
3. Put 1/3 of the beaten egg whites, egg yolks, butter, baking powder, liquid stevia, salt, and almond flour in a food processor and process until combined.
4. Stir in the remaining 2/3 of the egg whites and process until completely incorporated.
5. Pour mixture into the loaf pan and transfer in the oven.
6. Bake for about 30 minutes and dish out to serve hot.

Nutrition
Calories: 310
Carbs: 7.7g
Fats: 26g
Proteins: 12.4g
Sodium: 207mg
Sugar: 0.4g

• Macadamia Nut Bread

Serves: 5
Prep Time: 40 mins
This macadamia nut bread tastes just like traditional bread. This bread has a crusty outer layer and is soft inside!

Ingredients
- 5 large eggs
- 5 oz macadamia nuts
- ¼ cup coconut flour
- ½ teaspoon apple cider vinegar
- ½ teaspoon baking soda

Directions
1. Preheat oven to 350 degrees F and grease a standard-size bread pan.
2. Put macadamia nuts and eggs in a food processor and pulse until combined.
3. Add coconut flour, apple cider vinegar, and baking soda and pulse until incorporated.
4. Pour this mixture in the bread pan and transfer in the oven.
5. Bake for about 40 minutes and dish out to serve.

Nutrition
Calories: 299
Carbs: 8.3g
Fats: 27.1g
Proteins: 9.3g
Sodium: 197mg
Sugar: 1.7g

• Cauliflower Bread with Garlic & Herbs

Serves: 18
Prep Time: 1 hour
This cauliflower bread loaf with garlic and herbs makes a fabulous Keto garlic bread that is delicious and healthy.

Ingredients
- 10 large eggs, separated
- 1¼ cups coconut flour
- 3 cups cauliflower, finely chopped
- ¼ teaspoon cream of tartar
- 1½ tablespoons gluten-free baking powder
- 1 teaspoon sea salt
- 6 cloves garlic, minced
- 1 tablespoon fresh parsley, chopped
- 6 tablespoons butter, melted
- 1 tablespoon fresh rosemary, chopped

Directions
1. Preheat the oven to 350 degrees F and line a loaf pan with parchment paper.
2. Steam the riced cauliflower and keep aside to dry out completely.
3. Whisk together egg whites, and cream of tartar in a bowl and keep aside.
4. Place the baking powder, coconut flour, sea salt, egg yolks, butter, garlic, whipped egg whites and cauliflower in a food processor.
5. Process until combined and add in the parsley and rosemary.
6. Transfer the batter into the loaf pan and transfer in the oven.
7. Bake for about 50 minutes and slice to serve.

Nutrition
Calories: 115
Carbs: 7.4g
Fats: 7.5g
Proteins: 5.1g
Sodium: 372mg
Sugar: 0.6g

• **Keto Banana Walnut Bread**

Serves: 8
Prep Time: 1 hour 10 mins

This delicious and Ketogenic Banana Walnut Bread will leave you begging for more.

Ingredients

- 2 cups almond flour
- ½ cup walnuts
- Coconut oil, for greasing
- 3 medium bananas, sliced
- 3 large eggs
- ¼ cup olive oil
- 1 teaspoon baking soda

Directions

1. Preheat oven to 360 degrees F and grease a loaf pan with coconut oil.
2. Place all ingredients in a bowl and mix until well combined
3. Pour mixture into the loaf pan and transfer in the oven.
4. Bake for about 1 hour and slice to serve.

Nutrition

Calories: 333
Carbs: 17g
Fats: 27.5g
Proteins: 10.7g
Sodium: 186mg
Sugar: 6.6g

Possibly add
- flax seed meal
- inulin powder
- 1 tsp xantham gum

• Sesame Seed Keto Bread

Serves: 8
Prep Time: 55 mins
Baked to perfection, this sesame seed Keto bread is ideal for slicing as well as making toasts or sandwiches.

Ingredients
- 7 large eggs, separated
- 1 teaspoon baking powder
- 2 cups sesame seed flour
- ½ cup butter, melted

Directions
1. Preheat the oven to 355 degrees F and line a bread loaf tin with baking paper.
2. Whisk egg whites in a bowl and keep aside.
3. Mix together sesame seed flour, egg yolks, butter, and baking powder in another bowl.
4. Fold in the egg whites into sesame seed flour mixture until a uniform color is formed.
5. Pour the mixture in the bread loaf tin and transfer in the oven.
6. Bake for about 45 minutes and slice to serve.

Nutrition
Calories: 368
Carbs: 10g
Fats: 30g
Proteins: 17g
Sodium: 227mg
Sugar: 0.3g

• Fluffy Keto Buns

Serves: 4
Prep Time: 45 mins
If you love bread but not the carbs, these fabulous, fluffy Keto buns are totally for you!

Ingredients
- 2 tablespoons ground psyllium husks   *— flax seed meal ?*
- 2 egg yolks
- ½ tablespoon apple cider vinegar
- Salt and black pepper, to taste
- ¼ cup coconut flour
- 4 egg whites
- 1 teaspoon gluten free baking powder
- 1 cup water
- 1 teaspoon dried thyme
- 1 teaspoon dried oregano

Directions
1. Preheat the oven to 350 degrees and grease a baking sheet.
2. Whisk together eggs in a bowl and keep aside.
3. Mix together rest of the ingredients in another bowl and add whisked egg whites.
4. Form four rolls of equal size from the dough and arrange on the baking sheet.
5. Transfer in the oven and bake for about 40 minutes.
6. Remove from your oven and serve warm.

Nutrition
Calories: 86
Carbs: 8.7g
Fats: 3.1g
Proteins: 6g
Sodium: 237mg
Sugar: 0.3g

• Buttery Low Carb Flatbread

Serves: 4
Prep Time: 30 mins
Made with almond flour, coconut flour, and eggs, these are the best low-carb and grain-free flatbread substitute!

Ingredients
Wet Ingredients
- 2 tablespoons coconut flour
- 1 cup almond flour
- 2 teaspoons xanthan gum
- ½ teaspoon salt
- ½ teaspoon baking powder

Dry Ingredients
- 1 tablespoon olive oil
- 1 tablespoon water
- 1 tablespoon butter, melted
- 1 whole egg + 1 egg white

Directions
1. Preheat the oven to 375 degrees and grease a baking sheet.
2. Mix together the dry ingredients in a bowl until well combined.
3. Add the egg and egg white and fold gently into the flour mixture to form a dough.
4. Add water and mix the dough to allow the xanthan gum and flour to absorb the moisture.
5. Divide the dough in 4 equal parts and press each part to flatten.
6. Arrange the flatbread on the baking sheet and transfer in the oven.
7. Bake for about 20 minutes and dish out to serve.

Nutrition
Calories: 250
Carbs: 11g
Fats: 20.1g
Proteins: 8.7g
Sodium: 474mg
Sugar: 0.1g

• Garlic and Herb Focaccia Bread

Serves: 8
Prep Time: 30 mins
This grain free focaccia is seriously addictive. You will bake this again and again!

Ingredients
Wet Ingredients
- 1 tablespoon lemon juice
- 2 eggs
- 2 teaspoons olive oil + 2 tablespoons olive oil, to drizzle

Dry Ingredients
- 1 teaspoon flaky salt
- ½ teaspoon xanthan gum
- ¼ cup coconut flour
- 1 cup almond flour
- 1 teaspoon garlic powder
- ½ teaspoon baking soda
- ½ teaspoon baking powder

Directions
1. Preheat the oven to 350 degrees F and line a baking tray with parchment.
2. Mix together the dry ingredients in a bowl and keep aside.
3. Whisk together the wet ingredients until combined and mix with the dry ingredients.
4. Make a dough and flatten it with a spatula.
5. Arrange the focaccia on the baking tray and transfer in the oven.
6. Cover and bake for about 10 minutes.
7. Drizzle with olive oil and bake uncovered for about 15 more minutes.
8. Remove from the oven and serve warm.

Nutrition
Calories: 162
Carbs: 7g
Fats: 13.4g
Proteins: 5g
Sodium: 425mg
Sugar: 0.2g

• Coconut Bread

Serves: 5
Prep Time: 1 hour
Feel free to make it according to your own preference. Add nuts, raisins, coconut milk, or just make it plain.

Ingredients
- ¼ teaspoon salt
- ½ cup coconut flour
- ¼ teaspoon baking soda
- 6 eggs
- ¼ cup unsweetened almond milk
- ¼ cup coconut oil, melted

Directions
1. Preheat the oven to 350 degrees F and grease a loaf pan.
2. Mix together the coconut flour, baking soda and salt in a bowl.
3. Combine the eggs, milk, and coconut oil in another bowl.
4. Slowly add the wet ingredients into the dry ingredients and mix until combined.
5. Pour the mixture into the prepared loaf pan and transfer in the oven.
6. Bake for about 50 minutes and dish out to serve.

Nutrition
Calories: 219
Carbs: 8.5g
Fats: 17.5g
Proteins: 8.3g
Sodium: 262mg
Sugar: 0.4g

• Keto Mug Bread

Serves: 2
Prep Time: 15 mins
Try this easy and quick Keto and Paleo bread made in the oven in just 8 minutes with only 5 ingredients!

Ingredients
- ¼ cup almond flour
- 1 egg
- 1 tablespoon coconut flour
- 1 tablespoon coconut oil
- ¼ teaspoon baking powder

Directions
1. Preheat the oven to 350 degrees F and grease a mug.
2. Put all ingredients into a mug and mix with a fork until combined.
3. Transfer the mug in the oven and bake for about 8 minutes.
4. Serve immediately.

Nutrition
Calories: 190
Carbs: 6g
Fats: 16g
Proteins: 6.3g
Sodium: 36mg
Sugar: 0.2g

Chapter 8: Simple Cakes Recipes

• Buttery Chocolate Cake

Serves: 6
Prep Time: 1 hour
This buttery chocolate cake consumes time while making it, but it is very delicious when ready.

Ingredients
- 3½ oz. butter
- 7 oz. sugar-free dark chocolate
- 3½ oz. cream
- Erythritol, to taste
- 4 eggs, separated

Directions
1. Preheat the oven to 350 degrees F and grease a baking pan with some butter.
2. Mix the remaining butter with chocolate and microwave for about 2 minutes.
3. Add Erythritol, egg yolks, and cream to the chocolate mixture.
4. Whisk egg whites in another bowl until foamy and add to the creamy chocolate mixture.
5. Pour the batter into the baking pan and transfer in the oven.
6. Bake for about 45 minutes and remove from the oven.
7. Allow it cool for 5 minutes and then refrigerate it for about 4 hours to serve.

Nutrition
Calories: 173
Carbs: 9.4g
Fats: 16.2g
Proteins: 3.3g
Sodium: 42mg
Sugar: 0.2g

Italian Pecan Cake

Serves: 8
Prep Time: 1 hour

This is a quick and easy Italian Pecan Cake with the perfect combination of pecans and coconut.

Ingredients

Cake

- 1 cup Swerve
- 1 teaspoon vanilla essence
- ½ cup coconut, shredded
- ½ cup butter, softened
- 4 large eggs, separated
- ½ cup heavy cream
- ½ cup pecans, chopped
- 2 teaspoons baking powder
- 1½ cups almond flour
- ¼ teaspoon tartar cream
- ¼ cup coconut flour
- ½ teaspoon salt

Frosting

- ½ cup heavy whipping cream
- 1 teaspoon vanilla essence
- 8 ounces cream cheese, softened
- ½ cup butter, softened
- 1 cup powdered Swerve

Garnish

- 2 tablespoons pecans, chopped and lightly toasted
- 2 tablespoons coconut, shredded and lightly toasted

Directions

1. **Cake:** Preheat the oven to 330 degrees F and grease 2 baking pans of 8 inches each.
2. Whisk together egg yolks, butter, cream, Swerve, and vanilla essence in a bowl.
3. Combine almond flour, coconut flour, chopped pecans, baking powder, salt, and coconut.
4. Add the flour mixture to the egg yolk mixture and combine well.
5. Whisk together egg whites in a bowl until foamy and add this to the flour mixture.
6. Divide the mixture into the baking pans and transfer in the oven.
7. Bake for about 45 minutes and remove from the oven..
8. **Frosting:** Put all ingredients for frosting in a mixer and process until frothy.
9. Top the icing mixture over 1 cake and place the other cake over it.
10. Spread the rest of the icing on the top of the upper cake.
11. Garnish it with pecans and coconut.
12. Dish out to slice and serve.

Nutrition

Calories: 267

Fats: 44.5g

Sodium: 217mg

Carbs: 8.4g

Proteins: 3.1g

Sugar: 2.3g

Citrus Cream Cake

Serves: 4
Prep Time: 1 hour 15 mins
This is an easy citrus cream cake recipe. It is great for snacks!

Ingredients
For Cake
- 4 whole eggs
- 1¼ cups almond flour
- ¼ teaspoon lemon essence
- ¾ teaspoons baking powder
- ¾ teaspoons vanilla essence
- ¼ cup butter, unsalted softened
- ¾ cup erythritol
- ¼ teaspoon salt
- 4 ounces cream cheese

For Cream Frosting
- 1½ tablespoons heavy whipping cream
- 1/8 cup erythritol
- ¼ teaspoon vanilla essence

Directions
1. Preheat the oven to 350 degrees F and grease a baking pan.
2. Mix together butter, Erythritol, and cream cheese in a bowl.
3. Stir in eggs, vanilla essence, and lemon essence and mix well.
4. Whisk in baking powder, almond flour, and salt.
5. Pour the mixture into a baking pan and transfer in the oven.
6. Bake for about 1 hour and remove from the oven.
7. Mix together all ingredients for cream frosting in a bowl and spread on the cake.
8. Refrigerate the cake for about 1 hour and serve chilled.

Nutrition
Calories: 255
Carbs: 2.5g
Fats: 23.4g
Proteins: 7.9g
Sodium: 112mg
Sugar: 12.5g

Layered Cream Cake

Serves: 8
Prep Time: 45 mins
This recipe is forgiving. I eyeballed everything until it was exactly how I wanted it.

Ingredients
For Cream Cheese Icing:
- ½ cup butter, softened
- 2 tablespoons heavy cream
- 8 oz. cream cheese softened
- ½ cup powdered Swerve
- 1 teaspoon vanilla essence

For Carrot Cake Layers:
- ¾ cup Erythritol
- 14 tablespoons butter, melted
- ½ cup coconut flour
- 2 teaspoons baking powder
- 1¼ cups carrots, shredded
- 5 eggs large
- 2 teaspoons vanilla essence
- ¼ teaspoon unsweetened coconut, shredded
- ¼ teaspoon salt
- 1¾ cups almond flour
- 1½ teaspoons cinnamon, ground

Directions
1. **For Cream Cheese Icing:** Mix together all ingredients for the cream cheese icing until foamy and keep aside.
2. **For Carrot Cake Layers:** Preheat the oven to 350 degrees F and grease 2 baking pans.
3. Whisk together eggs with Erythritol in a bowl and keep aside.
4. Mix together almond flour, coconut flour, salt, cinnamon, and baking powder in another bowl.
5. Combine the two mixtures and stir in coconut, butter and carrots.
6. Divide the cake mixture into 2 baking pans and transfer in the oven.
7. Bake for about 30 minutes and remove from the oven to cool.
8. Top the icing mixture over 1 cake and place the other cake over it.
9. Spread the rest of the icing on the top of the upper cake.
10. Dish out to slice and serve.

Nutrition
Calories: 307

Fats: 29g

Sodium: 122mg

Carbs: 7g

Proteins: 6g

Sugar: 1g

Molten Lava Cake

Serves: 3
Prep Time: 20 mins
This Molten Chocolate Lava Cake is the perfect small batch dessert, which is incredibly easy to make and ready in less than 30 minutes.

Ingredients
- 2 ounces unsalted butter
- 2 tablespoons powdered Erythritol
- 4 fresh strawberries
- 2 ounces 70% dark chocolate
- 2 organic eggs
- 1 tablespoon almond flour

Directions
1. Preheat the oven to 350 degrees F and lightly grease 2 ramekins.
2. Mix chocolate with butter in a microwave-safe bowl and microwave for about 2 minutes.
3. Whisk together eggs in a bowl and add chocolate mixture, Erythritol, and almond flour until combined.
4. Divide the mixture evenly into 2 ramekins and transfer in the oven.
5. Bake for about 10 minutes and remove from the oven.
6. Keep aside for about 2 minutes and then invert the cakes carefully onto serving plates.
7. Garnish with the strawberries and serve.

Nutrition
Calories: 312
Carbs: 15.3g
Fats: 27.8g
Proteins: 5.5g
Sodium: 151mg
Sugar: 2.1g

Matcha Roll Cake

Serves: 10
Prep Time: 30 mins
This is a great dessert, especially nice for holidays, but it can be served anytime of the year.

Ingredients
For Cake:
- ½ cup powdered Swerve
- ¼ cup psyllium husk powder
- 1 cup almond flour
- ¼ cup matcha powder
- 1 teaspoon organic baking powder
- ½ teaspoon salt
- ½ cup heavy whipping cream
- 1 teaspoon organic vanilla extract
- 3 large organic eggs
- 4 tablespoons butter, melted

For Filling:
- 1 packet unflavored gelatin
- ¼ cup powdered Swerve
- 4 tablespoons water
- 2 cups heavy whipping cream
- 2 teaspoons organic vanilla extract

Directions
1. Preheat oven to 350 degrees F and lightly grease a baking sheet.
2. **For Cake:** Mix together almond flour, matcha powder, Swerve, baking powder, psyllium husk, and salt in a bowl.
3. Sift the almond flour mixture into a second bowl.
4. Combine rest of the ingredients in a bowl and mix with the almond flour mixture to form a thick dough.
5. Place the dough onto the baking sheet and roll into an even rectangle.
6. Transfer in the oven and bake for about 10 minutes.
7. Remove from the oven and allow to cool.
8. Roll the warm cake gently with the help of parchment paper and keep aside.
9. **For filling:** Put gelatin in water and microwave for about 20 seconds.
10. Remove from microwave and beat the gelatin mixture until smooth.

11. Place gelatin mixture and remaining ingredients in bowl and beat until cream becomes stiff.
12. Layer the whipped cream evenly over cooled cake and roll the cake gently.
13. Freeze for about 10 minutes and cut into desired sized slices to serve.

Nutrition
Calories: 257
Carbs: 13.1g
Fats: 22.5g
Proteins: 7.4g
Sodium: 194mg
Sugar: 6.2g

• **Allspice Almond Cake**

Serves: 8
Prep Time: 40 mins
This almond cake will impress your guests, and it is not as hard to make as it sounds.

Ingredients
For Cake:
- 5 tablespoons butter softened
- 2 tablespoons unsweetened almond milk
- 2 tablespoons coconut flour
- 1½ teaspoons cinnamon, ground
- ½ cup almonds

- ½ cup Erythritol
- 4 large eggs
- 1 teaspoon vanilla
- 1½ cups almond flour
- 1 tablespoon baking powder
- ¼ teaspoon ground allspice

For Cream Cheese Frosting:
- 2 tablespoons butter, softened
- ¼ cup Erythritol
- 4 oz. cream cheese, softened

- 1 teaspoon vanilla
- 1 tablespoon heavy cream

Directions
1. Preheat the oven to 350 degrees F and lightly grease a baking pan.
2. Mix erythritol with butter in a bowl until foamy.
3. Whisk in eggs, vanilla and milk and slowly add coconut flour, spices, almond flour, and baking powder.
4. Stir in the almonds to this mixture and pour this batter in the baking pan.
5. Transfer in the oven and bake for about 25 minutes.
6. Remove from the oven and place it over a wire rack.
7. Meanwhile, beat cream cheese frosting ingredients in a bowl until creamy.
8. Layer the frosting evenly over the cake and refrigerate for 30 minutes.
9. After ten minutes spread the frosting over the cake evenly.
10. Slice and serve to enjoy.

Nutrition
Calories: 331	Fats: 38.5g	Sodium: 283mg
Carbs: 9.2g	Proteins: 2.1g	Sugar: 3g

• Double Layer Cream Cake

Serves: 8
Prep Time: 45 mins
Fancy taste without all the work! This cake is wonderful for a get together or a special occasion.

Ingredients
First Layer
- ¼ cup Erythritol, powdered
- 1 tablespoon gelatin
- 2 large eggs
- 3 tablespoons coconut flour
- 1 teaspoon baking powder
- 8 tablespoons butter
- ½ teaspoon vanilla essence

Second Layer
- 8 oz. cream cheese
- 8 tablespoons butter
- ½ teaspoon vanilla essence
- 2 large eggs
- Liquid Stevia, to taste

Directions
1. Preheat the oven to 350 degrees F and lightly grease an 8-inch springform pan.
2. **First layer:** Whisk together eggs, vanilla and butter in a bowl and add gelatin, baking powder and coconut flour.
3. Combine well and keep this mixture aside.
4. **Second Layer:** Mix butter with cream cheese and add eggs, Stevia, and vanilla essence.
5. Beat well until the mixture is smooth.
6. Spread the first layer in the pan and top evenly with batter from the second layer.
7. Transfer in the oven and bake for about 25 minutes.
8. Remove from the oven and allow it to cool.
9. Refrigerate for about 3 hours in a wrapped plastic sheet and slice to serve.

Nutrition
Calories: 336
Carbs: 9.1g
Fats: 34.5g
Proteins: 5.1g
Sodium: 267mg
Sugar: 0.2g

Chunky Carrot Cake

Serves: 8
Prep Time: 45 mins
Even people who do not like carrot love this sweet and yummy cake.

Ingredients
- ¾ cup butter
- ½ teaspoon pineapple extract
- 2½ cups almond flour
- ½ teaspoon sea salt
- 1 cup pecans, chopped
- ¾ cup Erythritol
- 1 teaspoon vanilla essence
- 4 large eggs
- 2 teaspoons gluten-free baking powder
- 2 teaspoons cinnamon
- 2½ cups carrots, grated

Directions
1. Preheat the oven at 350 degrees F and grease two 9-inch baking dishes.
2. Mix Erythritol, cream, vanilla essence, and pineapple extract in a bowl.
3. Whisk in eggs one by one, then add cinnamon, baking powder, salt and flour to mix well.
4. Stir in pecans and carrots and divide the entire batter in the two pans.
5. Transfer in the oven and bake for about 30 minutes.
6. Remove the cakes from the pans and allow them to cool slightly.
7. Dish out to slice and serve.

Nutrition
Calories: 359
Carbs: 8.5g
Fats: 34g
Proteins: 7.5g
Sodium: 92mg
Sugar: 2g

Zesty Lemon Cake

Serves: 8
Prep Time: 1 hour
This is a moist and flavorful recipe that makes a large quantity of cake.

Ingredients
For Cake
- 5 eggs
- ½ cup coconut flour
- ¼ cup Swerve
- Juice from ½ lemon

- ½ teaspoon lemon zest
- ½ teaspoon salt
- ½ cup butter, melted
- ½ teaspoon xanthan gum

For Icing
- 3 tablespoons swerve
- ½ teaspoon lemon zest
- 1 cup cream cheese
- 1 teaspoon vanilla essence

Directions
1. Preheat the oven at 340 degrees F and grease a loaf pan.
2. Whisk egg whites using an electric mixer until it forms stiff peaks.
3. Mix together the remaining ingredients in another bowl and combine with egg whites.
4. Pour the batter to the loaf pan and transfer in the oven.
5. Bake for about 45 minutes and dish out.
6. Meanwhile, prepare the topping by beating icing ingredients in the electric mixer.
7. Place the baked cake on the wire rack and allow it to cool.
8. Layer the cream cheese icing over the cake and evenly spread it.
9. Refrigerate for about 30 minutes and cut into slices to enjoy.

Nutrition
Calories: 251

Carbs: 4.3g

Fats: 24.5g

Proteins: 5.9g

Sodium: 142mg

Sugar: 0.5g

Chapter 9: Perfect Cookies Recipes

• Chocolate Chip Butter Cookies

Serves: 8
Prep Time: 25 mins
Crisp edges and chewy middles, these delicious Chocolate Chip Butter Cookies are so easy to bake!

Ingredients
- ⅓ cup butter, unsalted
- 2 large eggs
- ⅛ teaspoon salt
- ¼ cup coconut flour
- 3 tablespoons Swerve
- 3 tablespoons sugar-free chocolate chips
- ¼ teaspoon vanilla essence

Directions
1. Preheat the oven at 350 degrees F and grease a cookie sheet.
2. Mix salt, Swerve and coconut flour in a bowl.
3. Beat the vanilla essence, butter, and eggs in a mixer.
4. Stir in the flour mixture to the eggs mixture to combine.
5. Add chocolate chips and spoon this mixture on a cookie sheet.
6. Bake the cookies in the oven for 15 minutes and allow it to cool before serving.

Nutrition
Calories: 198
Carbs: 4.5g
Fats: 19.2g
Proteins: 3.4g
Sodium: 142mg
Sugar: 3.3g

Buttery Energy Cookies

Serves: 8
Prep Time: 15 mins
I have been hounded to make these butter energy cookies repeatedly.

Ingredients
- 3 tablespoons butter
- 1 cup almond flour
- 2 tablespoons erythritol
- Pinch of salt
- 1 teaspoon vanilla essence

Directions
1. Preheat the oven at 350 degrees F and grease a cookie sheet.
2. Put all ingredients in a bowl and whisk until well combined.
3. Divide the cookie dough into small cookies and arrange on the cookie sheet.
4. Transfer the cookie sheet in the oven and bake for about 12 minutes.
5. Refrigerate to chill for about 1 hour and serve.

Nutrition
Calories: 114
Carbs: 3.1g
Fats: 9.6g
Proteins: 3.5g
Sodium: 155mg
Sugar: 1.4g

Cream Dipped Cookies

Serves: 8
Prep Time: 40 mins
This recipe makes very light and flaky cookies that are always requested for showers and weddings.

Ingredients
- ½ cup cacao nibs
- ½ cup almond butter
- 2 large eggs
- ¼ teaspoon salt
- 1 cup almond flour
- ½ cup coconut flakes, unsweetened
- 1/3 cup Erythritol
- ¼ cup butter, melted
- Stevia, to taste

Glaze:
- 1/8 teaspoon xanthan gum
- ½ teaspoon vanilla essence
- ¼ cup heavy whipping cream
- Stevia, to taste

Directions
1. Preheat the oven at 350 degrees F and grease a cookie sheet.
2. Combine all the dry ingredients in a bowl.
3. Beat eggs, Stevia almond butter, butter, and vanilla essence in another bowl.
4. Stir in the almond flour mixture and mix well.
5. Make cookies on a cookie sheet by dropping the batter with spoon.
6. Press each cookie to flatten it and transfer in the oven.
7. Bake for about 25 minutes and keep aside.
8. Combine the glaze ingredients in a saucepan and cook until the sauce thickens.
9. Once the cookies are done, pour this cooked glaze over the cookies equally.
10. Allow this glaze to set for about 15 minutes and enjoy.

Nutrition
Calories: 192
Carbs: 2.2g
Fats: 17.4g
Proteins: 4.7g
Sodium: 135mg
Sugar: 1.4g

• Keto Coconut Cookies

Serves: 18
Prep Time: 35 mins
Easy to make coconut cookies that are Keto friendly!

Ingredients
- ½ cup butter
- ½ tablespoon heavy cream
- 6 tablespoons coconut flour
- 1 teaspoon baking powder
- ½ teaspoon salt
- ¾ cup Splenda
- 3 eggs
- 1 teaspoon almond milk
- ½ cup unsweetened coconut flakes
- ¼ cup almond flour
- 1 teaspoon baking soda

Directions
1. Preheat the oven to 350 degrees F and grease lightly a baking sheet.
2. Mix together Splenda, butter, heavy cream, eggs, and almond milk in a bowl until smooth.
3. Combine coconut flakes, coconut flour, almond flour, baking powder, baking soda, and salt in another bowl.
4. Combine both mixtures until dough comes together.
5. Drop spoonfuls of cookie dough onto the baking sheet and transfer in the oven.
6. Bake for about 18 minutes and cool to serve.

Nutrition
Calories: 98   Fats: 8.9g   Sodium: 211mg
Carbs: 3.3g   Proteins: 2g   Sugar: 0g

Vanilla Cream Cheese Cookies

Serves: 8
Prep Time: 30 mins
Dough can be made days ahead. Frost with cream cheese icing when cool.

Ingredients
- 2 oz. plain cream cheese
- 2 teaspoons vanilla essence
- ¼ teaspoon sea salt
- ¼ cup butter
- ½ cup erythritol
- 1 large egg white
- 3 cups almond flour

Directions
1. Preheat the oven to 350 degrees F and grease lightly a cookie sheet.
2. Put butter, cream cheese, egg white, and vanilla essence in a blender and blend until smooth.
3. Add Erythritol, flour, and salt, and mix well until smooth.
4. Divide the dough into small cookies on the cookie sheet and transfer in the oven.
5. Bake for about 15 minutes and allow the cookies to cool to serve.

Nutrition
Calories: 195
Carbs: 4.5g
Fats: 14.3g
Proteins: 3.2g
Sodium: 125mg
Sugar: 0.5g

Peanut Butter Cookies

Serves: 6
Prep Time: 1 hour
These are so close to the packaged peanut butter cookies that you won't know the difference!

Ingredients
- ½ cup Swerve
- ½ cup peanut butter
- 1 egg

Directions
1. Preheat the oven to 350 degrees F and grease a baking sheet.
2. Mix together all ingredients in a bowl until thoroughly combined.
3. Scoop out dough with a cookie scoop and form balls.
4. Arrange on the baking sheet and press with a fork.
5. Transfer in the oven and bake for about 15 minutes.
6. Allow the cookies to cool for about 10 minutes.

Nutrition
Calories: 82
Carbs: 2.5g
Fats: 6g
Proteins: 3g
Sodium: 65mg
Sugar: 1g

• Coconut Vanilla Cookies

Serves: 4
Prep Time: 20 mins
Feel free to make it your own. Add nuts, raisins, coconut milk, or simply pain.

Ingredients
- ¾ teaspoon baking powder
- 1/6 cup coconut oil
- 2 large eggs
- ½ teaspoon vanilla essence
- 6 tablespoons coconut flour
- 1/8 teaspoon salt
- 3 tablespoons butter
- 6 tablespoons Swerve
- ½ tablespoon coconut milk

Directions
1. Preheat the oven to 375 degrees F and grease a cookie sheet.
2. Put all the wet ingredients in a food processor and process.
3. Stir in the remaining ingredients and mix well.
4. Divide the dough into small cookies and arrange on the cookie sheet.
5. Transfer in the oven and bake for about 10 minutes.
6. Allow the cookies to cool and serve.

Nutrition
Calories: 151
Carbs: 1.5g
Fats: 14.7g
Proteins: 0.8g
Sodium: 53mg
Sugar: 0.3g

• Cinnamon Snickerdoodle Cookies

Serves: 8
Prep Time: 25 mins

I received this recipe through a cookie exchange years ago, and it has become a favorite for family and friends.

Ingredients
Cookies:
- 2 teaspoons vanilla essence
- ½ cup almond milk
- 2 eggs
- 1 cup almond butter
- ¼ cup coconut oil, solid, at
- 1½ cups monk fruit sweetener
- 1 cup coconut flour
- 2 teaspoons tartar cream
- 1 teaspoon cinnamon
- 1¾ cups almond flour
- 1 teaspoon baking soda
- 1/8 teaspoon pink Himalayan salt

Topping:
- 1 tablespoon cinnamon
- 3 tablespoons monk fruit sweetener

Directions
1. Preheat the oven to 350 degrees F and grease a cookie sheet.
2. Add the wet ingredients of the cookies to a blender and beat well.
3. Stir in the dry mixture and combine well.
4. Place this batter in the refrigerator for 20 minutes to set.
5. Make small balls from this mixture.
6. Mix cinnamon and monk fruit in a shallow plate.
7. Roll these balls into this cinnamon mixture to coat well.
8. Place these balls on a baking sheet and transfer in the oven.
9. Bake for about 12 minutes and dish out to serve.

Nutrition
Calories: 252

Fats: 17.3g

Sodium: 153mg

Carbs: 7.2g

Proteins: 5.2g

Sugar: 0.3g

• Nutmeg Gingersnap Cookies

Serves: 8
Prep Time: 25 mins
This is a really a scrumptious recipe for Nutmeg Gingersnap Cookies. It is super easy and everyone loves it.

Ingredients
- ¼ cup butter, unsalted
- 1 teaspoon vanilla essence
- 2 cups almond flour
- 1 cup Erythritol
- 1 large egg
- ¼ teaspoon salt
- ¼ teaspoon nutmeg, ground
- ½ teaspoon cinnamon, ground
- 2 teaspoons ginger, ground
- ¼ teaspoon cloves, ground

Directions
1. Preheat the oven to 350 degrees F and grease a cookie sheet.
2. Beat the wet ingredients in an electric mixer.
3. Stir in the leftover ingredients and mix until smooth.
4. Divide the dough into small cookies and arrange on the cookie sheet spoon by spoon.
5. Transfer in the oven and bake for about 12 minutes.
6. Dish out to serve and enjoy.

Nutrition
Calories: 78
Carbs: 5.4g
Fats: 7.1g
Proteins: 2.3g
Sodium: 15mg
Sugar: 0.2g

• Vanilla Shortbread Cookies

Serves: 6
Prep Time: 25 mins
These homemade low carb Vanilla Shortbread Cookies are very easy to make and become downright simple.

Ingredients
- 6 tablespoons butter
- 1 teaspoon vanilla essence
- 2½ cups almond flour
- ½ cup erythritol

Directions
1. Preheat the oven to 350 degrees F and grease a cookie sheet.
2. Beat Erythritol with butter until frothy.
3. Stir in flour and vanilla essence while beating the mixture.
4. Divide this batter and arrange on a cookie sheet in small cookies.
5. Transfer in the oven and bake for about 15 minutes.
6. Dish out to serve and enjoy.

Nutrition
Calories: 288
Carbs: 9.6g
Fats: 25.3g
Proteins: 7.6g
Sodium: 74mg
Sugar: 0.1g

Chapter 10: Biscuits, Muffins and Scones Recipes

Cranberry Jalapeño "Cornbread" Muffins

Serves: 12
Prep Time: 40 mins

These are grain-free and low carb muffins that are made with coconut flour, cranberries, and jalapeños. They taste just like cornbread!

Ingredients
- 1/3 cup Swerve
- ½ teaspoon salt
- ½ cup butter, melted
- 1 cup fresh cranberries, cut in half
- 1 jalapeño, seeds removed, sliced into 12 slices, for garnish
- 1 cup coconut flour
- 1 tablespoon baking powder
- 7 large eggs, lightly beaten
- 1 cup unsweetened almond milk
- 3 tablespoons jalapeño peppers, minced
- ½ teaspoon vanilla extract

Directions
1. Preheat the oven to 330 degrees F and line muffin tins with parchment paper.
2. Whisk together Swerve, baking powder, coconut flour, and salt in a bowl thoroughly.
3. Add eggs, butter, vanilla extract, and almond milk and mix well.
4. Stir in jalapeños and cranberries and pour into the muffin tins.
5. Transfer in the oven and bake for about 30 minutes.
6. Dish out to serve and enjoy.

Nutrition
Calories: 160

Fats: 11.9g

Sodium: 236mg

Carbs: 8.6g

Proteins: 5.2g

Sugar: 0.6g

• Almond Flour Biscuits

Serves: 12
Prep Time: 25 mins
This recipe needs just 10 minutes' preparation and 5 common ingredients to make delicious biscuits.

Ingredients
- 2 teaspoons gluten-free baking powder
- 2 cups almond flour
- ½ teaspoons sea salt
- 1/3 cup butter
- 2 large eggs, beaten

Directions
1. Preheat the oven to 360 degrees F and grease a cookie sheet lightly.
2. Mix together dry ingredients in a large bowl and then add in the wet ingredients.
3. Scoop spoonfuls of the dough onto the cookie sheet and flatten with your fingers slightly.
4. Transfer in the oven and bake for about 15 minutes.
5. Allow to cool on the baking sheet and serve.

Nutrition
Calories: 165
Carbs: 4.2g
Fats: 15.3g
Proteins: 5.1g
Sodium: 255mg
Sugar: 0.7g

• Maple Nut Scones

Serves: 8
Prep Time: 50 mins
These Keto scones are the perfect evening snacks that your family will always demand.

Ingredients

- ½ cup coconut flour
- 2 tablespoons collagen
- 1 tablespoon baking powder
- 1½ cups almond flour
- ¼ cup Swerve
- ½ teaspoon salt
- 1 large egg

- 2½ tablespoons cold butter, cut into small pieces
- 1 teaspoon molasses
- ½ cup heavy cream
- 2 teaspoons maple extract
- 2/3 cup pecans, coarsely chopped

Maple Glaze Icing:

- 1 teaspoon maple extract
- 2 teaspoons water
- ½ cup powdered Erythritol 1 tablespoon half and half

Directions

1. Preheat the oven to 360 degrees F and grease a cookie sheet lightly.
2. Put the dry ingredients into the food processor and pulse until combined.
3. Add the egg, cream, butter, maple extract, molasses, and pecans to pulse again until the dough comes together into a ball.
4. Cut the dough into 8 wedges and arrange on the baking sheet with half an inch between the scones.
5. Transfer in the oven and bake for about 40 minutes.
6. Mix together the maple glaze ingredients and spread on the scones to serve.

Nutrition

Calories: 302	Fats: 27g	Sodium: 208mg
Carbs: 11g	Proteins: 7g	Sugar: 2g

Raspberry Muffins

Serves: 12
Prep Time: 15 mins
These delightful raspberry muffins will make a great innovation to any dinner table.

Ingredients
- 1 cup coconut milk
- 1 cup coconut butter
- ½ cup coconut oil
- 1 teaspoon vanilla essence
- Stevia, to taste
- ¼ cup cacao butter
- ¼ cup freeze-dried raspberries

Directions
1. Preheat the oven to 350 degrees F and grease muffin cups of a tray lightly
2. Put all the ingredients in a food processor and process until smooth.
3. Pour and divide the mixture into the muffin cups.
4. Transfer in the oven and bake for about 30 minutes.
5. Remove from the muffin cups and serve.

Nutrition
Calories: 261
Carbs: 6.1g
Fats: 27.1g
Proteins: 1.8g
Sodium: 10mg
Sugar: 2.1g

Keto Drop Biscuits

Serves: 6
Prep Time: 30 mins
Large Keto biscuits are very filling and substantial! Ultra tasty, tender, and moist!

Ingredients
- ½ cup coconut cream
- 2 tablespoons water
- ¼ cup psyllium husk, finely ground
- ¼ cup almond flour
- 1 teaspoon xanthan gum
- 7 tablespoons coconut oil
- 1 egg
- 2 teaspoons +1 tablespoon apple cider vinegar
- ¼ cup coconut flour
- 3½ teaspoons baking powder
- ½ teaspoon kosher salt

Directions
1. Preheat the oven to 450 degrees F and grease a baking tray.
2. Whisk together eggs, coconut cream, apple cider vinegar, and water in a medium bowl and keep aside.
3. Add almond flour, coconut flour, flaxseed meal, baking powder, whey protein, xanthan gum, and kosher salt to a food processor and pulse until combined.
4. Stir in the butter along with the egg mixture and pulse until combined.
5. Drop 6 parts of dough onto the baking tray and brush with the melted butter.
6. Transfer in the oven and bake for about 20 minutes.
7. Remove from the oven and serve cooled.

Nutrition
Calories: 245   Fats: 24.1g   Sodium: 257mg
Carbs: 12.2g   Proteins: 3.2g   Sugar: 0.7g

Blackberry Scones

Serves: 8
Prep Time: 30 mins
These scones are bursting with juicy fresh black berries and topped with natural blackberry glaze.

Ingredients
For Scones
- ¼ cup coconut flour
- ¼ teaspoon sea salt
- 1 cup blanched almond flour
- 3 tablespoons erythritol
- ½ teaspoon gluten-free baking powder
- ¼ cup unsweetened almond milk
- 1 large egg
- ½ cup blackberries
- 2 tablespoons coconut oil
- 1 teaspoon vanilla extract

For Glaze
- 1 teaspoon Erythritol
- 1 tablespoon coconut oil
- 2 tablespoons blackberries

Directions
1. Preheat the oven to 350 degrees F and grease a baking sheet.
2. Mix together coconut flour, almond flour, Erythritol, baking powder, and sea salt in a bowl.
3. Whisk together egg, coconut oil, vanilla extract, and almond milk in a small bowl.
4. Fold the blackberries into the dough and place the dough onto the baking sheet.
5. Cut into 8 wedges and transfer in the oven.
6. Bake for about 20 minutes until golden and remove from oven to keep aside.
7. Meanwhile, puree the glaze ingredients in a blender and drizzle over the scones to serve.

Nutrition
Calories: 159	Fats: 13g	Sodium: 200mg
Carbs: 8g	Proteins: 5g	Sugar: 3g

Lemon Muffins

Serves: 6
Prep Time: 35 mins
You will love this easy blackberry scones recipe, as it makes highly palatable and mouthwatering muffins.

Ingredients
- ¼ cup golden flax meal
- 2 tablespoons poppy seeds
- ¾ cup almond flour
- 1/3 cup Erythritol
- 1 teaspoon organic baking powder
- ¼ cup heavy cream
- ¼ cup salted butter, melted
- 1 teaspoon organic vanilla extract
- 2 teaspoons fresh lemon zest, finely grated
- 3 large organic eggs
- 3 tablespoons fresh lemon juice
- 20 drops liquid Stevia

Directions
1. Preheat the oven to 350 degrees F and grease 6 cups of a muffin tin.
2. Mix together the flax meal, flour, poppy seeds, baking powder, and Erythritol in a bowl.
3. Whisk the eggs, heavy cream and butter in another bowl and mix with the flour mixture.
4. Add lemon juice, vanilla extract, lemon zest, and Stevia and mix well.
5. Pour the mixture evenly into the muffin cups and transfer in the oven.
6. Bake for about 20 minutes and remove from oven.
7. Allow to cool for about 10 minutes and serve.

Nutrition
Calories: 249	Fats: 21.7g	Sodium: 99mg
Carbs: 14.5g	Proteins: 7.9g	Sugar: 14.2g

• Cheesy Keto Biscuits

Serves: 4
Prep Time: 30 mins
These cheesy delicious low carb biscuits will become your favorite!

Ingredients
- 1 tablespoon baking powder
- 2 cups almond flour
- 2½ cups Cheddar cheese, shredded
- ¼ cup half-and-half
- 4 eggs

Directions
1. Preheat the oven to 350 degrees F and grease a baking sheet.
2. Mix together almond flour and baking powder in a large bowl.
3. Stir in Cheddar cheese and form a small well in the center of the bowl.
4. Add eggs and half-and-half to the center and mix well until a sticky batter forms.
5. Drop small portions of batter onto the baking sheet and transfer in the oven.
6. Bake for about 20 minutes and dish out to serve.

Nutrition
Calories: 329
Carbs: 7.2g
Fats: 27.1g
Proteins: 16.7g
Sodium: 391mg
Sugar: 1g

• Keto Scones with Bacon

Serves: 6
Prep Time: 35 mins
These Keto scones are made savory with the addition of delicious bacon.

Ingredients
- 1½ teaspoons baking soda
- 3 cups almond flour
- ½ teaspoon kosher salt
- 2 large eggs
- 2 tablespoons apple cider vinegar
- 8 slices bacon, diced and cooked until crisp
- 4 tablespoons cold butter, cut into cubes
- 2 tablespoons bacon grease

Directions
1. Preheat the oven to 350 degrees F and grease lightly a baking sheet.
2. Mix together the almond flour, baking soda, and kosher salt in a large bowl.
3. Stir in the cold butter and mix well.
4. Whisk together the eggs, vinegar, and bacon grease in another bowl and add to the flour mixture.
5. Mix well and cut triangles from the dough.
6. Cut into 6 triangles and arrange onto the baking sheet.
7. Transfer in the oven and bake for about 25 minutes to serve.

Nutrition
Calories: 510
Carbs: 12g
Fats: 46g
Proteins: 18g
Sodium: 93mg
Sugar: 2.2g

Blueberry Muffins

Serves: 12
Prep Time: 35 mins
Everyone will love these blueberry muffins. It is great as a breakfast muffin, snack, or with a meal.

Ingredients
- ½ cup Swerve
- ¼ teaspoon salt
- ¼ cup butter, melted
- ¾ cup fresh blueberries
- 2 cups almond flour
- 2 teaspoons organic baking powder
- 3 organic eggs, beaten
- ¼ cup unsweetened almond milk
- 1 teaspoon organic vanilla extract

Directions
1. Preheat the oven to 350 degrees F and grease 12 cups of a muffin tin.
2. Mix together almond flour, salt, Swerve, and baking powder in a bowl.
3. Whisk together the eggs, almond milk, butter, and vanilla extract in another bowl.
4. Combine the egg mixture well with the flour mixture and add blueberries.
5. Pour the mixture evenly into prepared muffin cups and transfer in the oven.
6. Bake for about 20 minutes and remove from the oven.
7. Allow to cool for about 10 minutes and serve.

Nutrition
Calories: 170
Carbs: 5.9g
Fats: 13.9g
Proteins: 5.5g
Sodium: 104mg
Sugar: 1g

Chapter 11: Easy Tarts and Bars Recipes

◆ Mixed Berries Tart

Serves: 8
Prep Time: 25 mins
This free-form mixed berries tart is thickly glazed and beautiful. Be sure to use perfectly ripe, sweet mixed berries.

Ingredients
Tart crust:
- ¼ cup Erythritol, powdered
- ¼ teaspoon sea salt
- 2¼ cups almond flour
- 5 tablespoons butter, melted

Filling:
- 2 tablespoons erythritol
- 6 oz. mascarpone cheese
- 1/3 cup heavy cream
- ¼ teaspoon lemon zest
- 1 teaspoon vanilla essence

To garnish:
- 6 blueberries
- 6 raspberries
- 6 blackberries

Directions
1. **Crust:** Preheat the oven to 350 degrees F and grease 8 small tart pans with butter.
2. Put butter, almond flour, Erythritol, and salt in a food processor and process until coarse.
3. Divide this mixture into the tart pans and press firmly.
4. Transfer in the oven and bake for about 10 minutes.
5. **Filling:** Put the erythritol and cream in an electric mixer and beat for about 2 minutes.
6. Stir in the cream, lemon zest, and vanilla essence slowly and continue beating until the mixture thickens.
7. Fill this mixture in the baked crust of each tart pan and garnish with the berries.
8. Chill for 10 minutes in the refrigerator to serve and enjoy.

Nutrition
Calories: 237
Carbs: 5g
Fats: 22g
Proteins: 5g
Sodium: 118mg
Sugar: 1g

• Crunchy Chocolate Bars

Serves: 8
Prep Time: 15 mins
These are fantastic Crunchy Chocolate Bars. You've got to try them!

Ingredients
- 1 cup almond butter
- 1½ cups sugar-free chocolate chips
- Stevia, to taste
- 3 cups pecans, chopped
- ¼ cup coconut oil

Directions
1. Preheat the oven to 350 degrees F and grease an 8-inch baking pan.
2. Melt chocolate chips with stevia and coconut oil in a glass bowl.
3. Mix well and add seeds and nuts.
4. Pour this nutty batter into the baking pan and transfer in the oven.
5. Bake for about 10 minutes and remove from the oven to cool.
6. Place the pan in the refrigerator for about 3 hours.
7. Dish out and slice into small bars to serve.

Nutrition
Calories: 316
Carbs: 8.3g
Fats: 30.9g
Proteins: 6.4g
Sodium: 8mg
Sugar: 1.8g

Creamy Chocolate Tart

Serves: 8
Prep Time: 40 mins
Bring this treat to a picnic, and your friends will ask which bakery it came from.

Ingredients
Crust
- 2 tablespoons Erythritol
- 6 tablespoons coconut flour
- 4 tablespoons butter, melted
- 1 large egg
- 2 (4-inch) tart pans

Filling
- ½ cup heavy whipping cream
- 2 oz. sugar-free chocolate
- ¼ cup Erythritol, powdered
- 1 large egg
- Liquid Stevia, to taste
- 1 oz. cream cheese

Directions
1. Preheat the oven to 350 degrees F and grease 2 (4 inches) tart pans with butter.
2. Put all the ingredients for the crust in a food processor and process until coarse.
3. Divide this mixture into each tart pan and press firmly.
4. Pierce few holes in the crusts with a fork and transfer in the oven.
5. Bake both the crusts for about 12 minutes.
6. Meanwhile, heat cream in a saucepan on medium heat and add chocolate.
7. Cook until it melts and transfer in an immersion blender.
8. Puree this mixture and add egg, cream cheese, Erythritol, and Stevia.
9. Divide this filling into each crust and return both the pans to the oven.
10. Bake for about 15 minutes and allow to cool.
11. Transfer to the refrigerator for about 3 hours to serve chilled.

Nutrition
Calories: 190
Carbs: 5.5g

Fats: 17.2g
Proteins: 3g

Sodium: 28mg
Sugar: 2.8g

• Lemon Egg Bars

Serves: 8
Prep Time: 1 hour
Nothing prepares you for this intense, awesome, sweet-tart lemon egg flavor.

Ingredients
- 1¾ cups almond flour
- ½ cup butter, melted
- 1 cup Erythritol, powdered
- 3 large eggs
- 3 medium lemons, juiced

Directions
1. Preheat the oven to 350 degrees F and grease an 8-inch baking pan.
2. Whisk together butter, almond flour, Erythritol, and salt in a bowl.
3. Transfer this mixture to a pan and press firmly.
4. Place in the oven and bake for about 20 minutes.
5. Dish out and allow it to cool for 10 minutes at room temperature.
6. Mix the rest of the ingredients in a separate bowl and spread evenly over the baked crust.
7. Bake again for 25 minutes in the oven and slice the bars after removing from oven.
8. Serve and enjoy.

Nutrition
Calories: 282
Carbs: 9.4g
Fats: 25.1g
Proteins: 8g
Sodium: 117mg
Sugar: 0.7g

Blackberry Lemon Tart

Serves: 8
Prep Time: 30 mins
Your family will love this tart. You can garnish it with blackberries and lime zest.

Ingredients
- 2 (9" tart molds with loose bottoms)
- 1 tablespoon sliced almonds
- 1 cup blackberries
- 1 cup lemon curd

Almond Flour Pie Crust
- ½ cup coconut flour
- 4 tablespoons cold butter, unsalted
- 1½ cups almond flour
- 4 tablespoons Erythritol, powdered
- 2 eggs

Directions
1. Preheat the oven to 350 degrees F and grease two tart molds.
2. Mix together all the ingredients for almond flour pie crust to form a dough.
3. Divide the dough into two equal sized balls and place in the tart molds.
4. Make a few holes into each dough layer with a fork and transfer in the oven.
5. Bake for about 15 minutes and remove from the oven to cool.
6. Fill both the crusts equally with lemon curd and top with berries, Erythritol, and almond slices.
7. Serve and enjoy.

Nutrition
Calories: 321
Carbs: 8.1g
Fats: 12.9g
Proteins: 5.4g
Sodium: 28mg
Sugar: 1.8g

Caramel Bars

Serves: 8
Prep Time: 55 mins
These chewy and crispy caramel bars will be a new family favorite treat!

Ingredients
For the Cracker Base:
- 1 cup almond flour
- ¼ teaspoon salt
- ¼ teaspoon baking powder
- 1 egg
- 2 tablespoons grass-fed salted butter, melted

Caramel Sauce:
- ½ cup butter
- ½ cup Swerve
- ½ cup heavy cream
- 1 teaspoon caramel extract
- ¼ teaspoon salt
- ½ teaspoon vanilla essence

Toppings:
- 1 cup pecans, chopped
- 2 cups chocolate chips
- 1 cup coconut, shredded

Directions
1. **Crackers:** Preheat the oven to 300 degrees F and grease a baking pan.
2. Combine baking powder, salt, and almond flour in a bowl.
3. Whisk eggs and butter in a bowl and combine with the flour mixture.
4. Place the dough on the working surface layered with parchment paper.
5. Cut the dough into a rectangle then cover it with a parchment paper.
6. Spread it using a rolling pin into 1/8 inch thick dough sheet.
7. Transfer it to the baking pan and bake for about 35 minutes.
8. Increase the temperature of the oven to 375 degrees F.
9. **Caramel sauce:** Put butter, Swerve, vanilla, cream, and caramel extracts in a saucepan.
10. Combine well and spread the sauce over the baked crackers base.
11. Drizzle chocolate chips, coconut, and pecans over it and transfer in the oven.
12. Bake for another 5 minutes and remove from the pan.
13. Allow it to cool and slice to serve.

Nutrition
Calories: 358   Fats: 35.2g   Sodium: 178mg
Carbs: 7.4g   Proteins: 5.5g   Sugar: 1.1g

Strawberry Vanilla Tart

Serves: 3
Prep Time: 25 mins
A lovely multi-season tart using fresh strawberries, coconut flour, and a hint of vanilla!

Ingredients
Coconut crust:
- ¾ cup coconut flour
- ½ cup coconut oil
- 2 eggs

- 1 teaspoon powdered sweetener
- 1 teaspoon vanilla essence

Cream Filling:
- 2 eggs, separated
- 1 cup strawberries
- 1 cup mascarpone

- 1 teaspoon vanilla essence
- 2 tablespoons Stevia, powdered

Directions
1. **Crust:**
2. Preheat the oven to 350 degrees F and grease a baking pan.
3. Whisk together eggs in a bowl and add rest of the ingredients.
4. Spread this dough in between two sheets of parchment paper.
5. Place this dough sheet in a greased pan and pierce holes in it with a fork.
6. Transfer in the oven and bake for about 10 minutes.
7. **Cream Filling:**
8. Whisk the egg whites in an electric mixer until frothy.
9. Stir in mascarpone cream, egg yolks, sweetener, and vanilla and beat for about 3 minutes.
10. Spread this filling evenly in the baked crust and top with Stevia and strawberries.
11. Place the pie in the refrigerator for about 30 minutes and serve hot.

Nutrition
Calories: 236
Carbs: 7.6g

Fats: 21.5g
Proteins: 4.3g

Sodium: 21mg
Sugar: 1.4g

Peanut Butter Bars

Serves: 8
Prep Time: 15 mins
Since they keep in the freezer for months, I love to grab them straight from the freezer and pack them for picnic snacks.

Ingredients
Bars
- 2 oz. butter
- ¾ cup almond flour
- ¼ cup Swerve
- ½ teaspoon vanilla extract
- ½ cup peanut butter

Topping
- ½ cup sugar-free chocolate chips

Directions
1. Preheat the oven to 300 degrees F and grease a baking pan.
2. Put all the ingredients for the bars in a bowl and mix well.
3. Spread this mixture in the pan and top with chocolate chips.
4. Transfer in the oven and bake for about 15 minutes.
5. Remove from the oven and transfer the pan in the refrigerator for about 1 hour.
6. Remove the base from pan and slice to serve.

Nutrition
Calories: 214
Carbs: 6.5g
Fats: 19g
Proteins: 6.5g
Sodium: 123mg
Sugar: 1.9g

Cheesecake Jam Tarts

Serves: 6
Prep Time: 45 mins
Very, very easy to make! They'll be beloved by both kids and adults!

Ingredients
Crust
- ½ cup almond flour
- 1½ tablespoons butter, melted

Filling
- 1 small egg
- ½ teaspoon vanilla essence
- 1/8 teaspoon salt
- 6 oz. cream cheese
- 1/8 cup Erythritol
- ½ tablespoon fresh lemon juice

Toppings
- 1/8 cup strawberry jam, sugar-free
- 1/8 cup blueberries

Directions
1. Preheat the oven to 340 degrees F and grease muffin tins.
2. Mix butter and almond flour in a bowl and pour this mixture into the muffin tin.
3. Transfer in the oven and bake for about 8 minutes.
4. Meanwhile, beat cream cheese in an electric mixture along with an egg.
5. Stir in Erythritol, vanilla essence, salt, and lemon juice and combine well.
6. Divide this filling into the muffin crust and transfer in the oven.
7. Bake the tarts for 20 minutes and allow it to cool after removing from oven.
8. Top with jam and blueberries and refrigerate overnight to serve.

Nutrition
Calories: 175   Fats: 16g   Sodium: 8mg
Carbs: 2.8g   Proteins: 9g   Sugar: 1.8g

Chocolate Dipped Granola Bars

Serves: 4
Prep Time: 35 mins
This is one of my favorite bars of all time. They serve as the best dessert with dinner.

Ingredients
- 3 tablespoons coconut oil
- 1 oz. sesame seeds
- 1½ oz. walnuts
- 1 oz. pumpkin seeds
- 1 teaspoon cinnamon, ground
- 1½ oz. sugar-free dark chocolate
- 1 egg
- 1½ oz. almonds
- ¼ teaspoon flaxseed
- 1 oz. coconut, shredded, unsweetened
- 1 oz. sugar-free dark chocolate
- 2 tablespoons tahini
- ½ pinch sea salt
- ½ teaspoon vanilla essence

Directions
1. Preheat the oven to 340 degrees F and grease a baking pan.
2. Put all the ingredients in a food processor, except chocolate, and coarsely grind.
3. Spread the ground mixture in the baking pan and transfer in the oven.
4. Bake for about 20 minutes and remove from oven.
5. Allow it to cool at room temperature and slice it into small squares.
6. Melt the chocolate in a microwave and pour over the bars.
7. Arrange the bars over a baking sheet and refrigerate them for about 30 minutes to serve.

Nutrition
Calories: 313   Fats: 28.4g   Sodium: 39mg
Carbs: 9.2g   Proteins: 8.1g   Sugar: 3.1g

Chapter 12: Tasty Pies Recipes

• Pumpkin Almond Pie

Serves: 8
Prep Time: 1 hour 15 mins
This Pumpkin Almond Pie goes perfectly with your favorite soup or as a snack.

Ingredients
Almond Flour Pie Crust
- 4 tablespoons butter, melted
- 2 cups almond flour
- 1 teaspoon vanilla
- ½ teaspoon cinnamon
- 1 egg yolk

Pumpkin Spice Filling
- 1 cup heavy cream
- 2 teaspoons pumpkin pie spice
- ⅔ cups Swerve
- 8 ounces cream cheese
- 4 eggs
- 1 teaspoon vanilla
- ¼ teaspoon salt

Directions
1. Preheat the oven to 400 degrees F and grease a pie pan.
2. Mix together all the ingredients for the crust in a bowl and transfer into the pie pan.
3. Press this mixture and transfer into the oven.
4. Bake this crust for about 12 minutes and keep aside.
5. **Filling:** Whisk together eggs and cream cheese until it turns frothy.
6. Add rest of the ingredients and stir well to combine.
7. Spread this filling evenly into the baked crust and return the stuffed pie to the oven.
8. Bake for another 45 minutes and allow to cool for 10 minutes.
9. Slice and enjoy.

Nutrition
Calories: 285

Carbs: 3.5g

Fats: 27.3g

Proteins: 7.2g

Sodium: 165mg

Sugar: 0.4g

Key Lime Pie

Serves: 8
Prep Time: 40 mins
Creamy and tangy Key Lime Pie makes a delightful summer dessert.

Ingredients
For Crust:
- ½ cup coconut flour, sifted
- ¼ cup butter, melted
- ¼ teaspoon salt
- ½ cup almond flour
- ¼ cup Erythritol
- 2 organic eggs

For Filling:
- ½ cup Erythritol
- 2 teaspoons xanthan gum
- 3 organic egg yolks
- 2 tablespoons unsweetened dried coconut
- ¾ cup unsweetened coconut milk
- ¼ cup heavy cream
- 1 teaspoon guar gum
- ¼ teaspoon powdered Stevia
- ½ cup key lime juice

For Topping:
- ½ lime, cut into slices
- 1 cup whipped cream

Directions
1. Preheat the oven to 390 degrees F and grease a 9-inch pie dish.
2. **For crust:** Mix together all ingredients in a bowl to form a dough.
3. Arrange the dough between 2 sheets of wax paper and roll into 1/8-inch thick circle.
4. Place the dough in the pie dish and press firmly.
5. Pierce the bottom and sides of crust with a fork at many places.
6. Transfer in the oven and bake for about 10 minutes.
7. Remove from the oven and allow it to cool.
8. Reset the oven to 350 degrees F.
9. **For filling:** Put coconut milk, heavy cream, egg yolks, lime juice, erythritol, guar gum, xanthan gum and Stevia in a food processor.
10. Pulse until well combined and spread the filling mixture evenly over crust.
11. Transfer in the oven and bake for about 10 minutes.
12. Remove from oven and allow to cool for about 10 minutes.
13. Freeze for about 4 hours and top with whipped cream and lime slices to serve.

Nutrition
Calories: 255

Fats: 24.8g

Sodium: 147mg

Carbs: 13.1g

Proteins: 5.2g

Sugar: 8.9g

Meringue Pie

Serves: 10
Prep Time: 1 hour
This is a traditional lemon meringue pie that is made entirely from scratch.

Ingredients
- 2 tablespoons coconut flour
- 1 tablespoon granulated Swerve
- ¼ teaspoon salt
- 4 tablespoons ice water
- 1¼ cups almond flour
- 2 tablespoons arrowroot starch
- 1 teaspoon xanthan gum
- 5 tablespoons chilled butter, cut into small pieces

For Filling:
- 1½ cups plus 2 tablespoons water, divided
- ¼ teaspoon salt
- 3 tablespoons butter
- 1 tablespoon grass-fed gelatin
- 4 large organic egg yolks
- 1 cup granulated Swerve
- 2 teaspoons fresh lemon zest, grated
- 1/3 cup fresh lemon juice
- ½ teaspoon xanthan gum

For Meringue Topping:
- ¼ teaspoon cream of tartar
- ¼ cup powdered Swerve
- ½ teaspoon organic vanilla extract
- 4 large organic egg whites
- Pinch of salt
- ¼ cup granulated Swerve

Directions
1. Preheat the oven to 335 degrees F and grease a pie pan.
2. **For crust:** Put the flours, butter, arrowroot starch, Swerve, xanthan gum, and salt in a food processor until combined.
3. Add ice water slowly to form a dough and transfer into a pie pan.
4. Press gently and pierce holes in the crust with a fork.

5. Transfer in the oven and bake for about 12 minutes.
6. Remove from the oven and keep aside to cool completely.
7. Reheat the oven to 300 degrees F.
8. **For filling:** Whisk together egg yolks in a bowl and slowly add ½ cup of water, beating until well combined.
9. Boil Swerve, salt and lemon zest in 1 cup of the water in a pan.
10. Whisk in the egg yolks mixture slowly into the pan, beating continuously.
11. Lower the heat and cook for about 1 minute, stirring continuously.
12. Remove from the heat and stir in the butter and lemon juice until smooth.
13. Top with xanthan gum and beat vigorously with a wire whisk until well combined.
14. Meanwhile, dissolve the gelatin into remaining 2 tablespoons of water in a small bowl.
15. Keep aside for about 2 minutes and add the gelatin mixture into hot lemon mixture.
16. Beat until well combined and cover the pan to keep aside.
17. **For topping:** Whisk together the egg whites, cream of tartar, and salt in a large bowl and beat until frothy.
18. Add the powdered Swerve, granulated Swerve, and vanilla extract slowly until stiff peaks form.
19. Pour the warm filling evenly over the crust and top with meringue.
20. Transfer in the oven and bake for about 20 minutes.
21. Remove from the oven and keep aside to cool.
22. Refrigerate for at least 3 hours and serve chilled.

Nutrition
Calories: 215
Carbs: 7.2g
Fats: 18.5g
Proteins: 6.7g
Sodium: 159mg
Sugar: 1.1g

Keto Meat Pie

Serves: 8
Prep Time: 25 mins

Meat pie is great for packed lunches. It sounds a little old-school, but you can rediscover its deliciousness with this recipe.

Ingredients
The Filling
- 1 garlic clove, finely chopped
- 20 oz. ground beef
- 1 tablespoon dried oregano
- ½ cup water
- ½ yellow onion, finely chopped
- 2 tablespoons butter
- Salt and black pepper, to taste
- 4 tablespoons tomato paste

Pie Crust
- 4 tablespoons sesame seeds
- 1 tablespoon ground psyllium husk powder
- 1 pinch salt
- 4 tablespoons water
- ¾ cup almond flour
- 4 tablespoons coconut flour
- 1 teaspoon baking powder
- 3 tablespoons olive oil
- 1 egg

Topping
- 7 oz. cheddar cheese, shredded
- 8 oz. cottage cheese

Directions
1. Preheat the oven to 350 degrees F and grease a springform pan.
2. Heat olive oil in a pan and add onion and garlic.
3. Sauté for about 3 minutes and add ground beef, dried oregano, salt and black pepper.
4. Cook for about 4 minutes and add tomato paste, psyllium husk powder and water.

5. Lower the heat and allow to simmer for at least 20 minutes.
6. Meanwhile, make the dough for the crust by mixing all the dough ingredients in a food processor.
7. Spread the dough in the pan and transfer in the oven.
8. Bake for about 15 minutes and remove from the oven.
9. Fill the meat in the crust and top with cheese.
10. Transfer in the oven and bake for about 40 minutes.
11. Serve hot.

Nutrition
Calories: 467
Carbs: 12.7g
Fats: 30.5g
Proteins: 36.9g
Sodium: 368mg
Sugar: 2.4g

Keto Silk Pie

Serves: 4
Prep Time: 15 mins

Serve lukewarm for peak flavor. Any cook can get rave reviews from this easy and delicious recipe.

Ingredients
For the crust:
- ½ teaspoon baking powder
- 1/3 cup granulated Stevia
- 1½ teaspoons vanilla extract
- 1½ cups almond flour
- 1/8 teaspoon salt
- 3 tablespoons butter
- 1 medium egg
- 1 teaspoon butter, for greasing the pan

For the filling:
- 4 tablespoons sour cream
- ½ cup + 2 teaspoons granulated Stevia
- 16 oz. cream cheese, room temperature
- 4 tablespoons butter
- 1 tablespoon +1 teaspoon vanilla extract
- ½ cup cocoa powder
- 1 cup whipping cream

Directions
1. Preheat the oven to 375 degrees F and grease a 9-inch pie pan with some butter.
2. Combine baking powder, almond flour, salt, and 1/3 cup Stevia in a bowl and add butter.
3. Stir in egg and vanilla extract and knead until the dough forms into a ball.
4. Transfer the dough into the pie pan and spread it covering the bottom and sides of the pan.
5. Pierce the holes in the crust and transfer in the oven.
6. Bake for about 15 minutes and remove crust from the oven to cool.
7. **For the filling:** Place sour cream, cream cheese, butter, vanilla extract, cocoa powder, and ½ cup stevia in a blender.

8. Blend until fluffy and place the whipping cream in a separate bowl.
9. Add 2 teaspoons granulated stevia and 1 teaspoon vanilla extract to the cream and beat to form stiff peaks.
10. Mix the whipped cream mixture into the sour cream mixture.
11. Scoop this mixture into the crust and cover to refrigerate for at least 3 hours before serving.

Nutrition
Calories: 449
Carbs: 9.3g
Fats: 43.6g
Proteins: 9.5g
Sodium: 267mg
Sugar: 2.3g

Banana Cream Pie

Serves: 10
Prep Time: 45 mins
This low carb banana cream pie has three basic steps to assemble!

Ingredients
Crust
- 1 batch Low Carb Walnut Pie Crust

Banana Cream Filling
- 1/3 cup almond milk
- 1/8 teaspoon xanthan gum
- 2 large eggs
- 1 teaspoon banana extract
- ½ teaspoon Stevia
- 1 cup heavy cream
- 1/3 cup Erythritol
- 2 tablespoons cornstarch
- 3 large egg yolks
- 1 teaspoon vanilla
- 1 pinch salt
- 2 tablespoons butter

For Filling and Topping
- Stevia, to taste
- 1½ cups heavy cream

Directions
1. Preheat the oven to 325 degrees F and grease a 9-inch pie pan.
2. **Banana Cream Filling:** Mix together all the ingredients in a saucepan on medium-low heat.
3. Allow to simmer and remove from heat.
4. Refrigerate overnight and fill in the readymade low carb crust.
5. Transfer it in the oven and bake for about 20 minutes.
6. Dish out and keep aside.
7. Mix Stevia in heavy cream and pour over the pie.
8. Refrigerate at least 4 hours before serving.

Nutrition
Calories: 478
Carbs: 9g
Fats: 47g
Proteins: 9g
Sodium: 145mg
Sugar: 3.8g

Chayote Squash Mock Apple Pie

Serves: 16
Prep Time: 1 hour
Enjoy this fantastic and delicious low carb chayote squash mock apple pie without any guilt, as it is Keto and gluten-free.

Ingredients
Crust
- 1½ cups almond flour
- ½ teaspoon salt
- ½ cup butter, melted
- ¾ cup coconut flour
- 4 eggs
- 1 tablespoon whole psyllium husks

Filling
- ¾ cup stevia
- ¼ teaspoon ginger
- 1 tablespoon lemon juice
- 1/3 cup butter cut in small pieces
- 5 medium chayote squash, peeled and sliced
- 1½ teaspoons cinnamon
- 1/8 teaspoon nutmeg
- 1 tablespoon xanthan gum
- 2 teaspoons apple extract

Topping
- 1 tablespoon Stevia
- 1 egg

Directions
1. Preheat the oven to 375 degrees F and grease a 9-inch pie pan.
2. Mix together crust ingredients to form a dough ball.
3. Transfer the dough ball into the pie dish and press firmly.
4. **Filling:** Boil sliced chayote and drain completely.
5. Add Stevia, apple extract, lemon juice, and xanthan gum to cooked chayote squash.
6. Pour chayote mixture into pie pan and top with butter.
7. **Topping:** Brush egg on pie top and sprinkle with Stevia.
8. Bake for about 35 minutes and dish out to serve.

Nutrition
Calories: 187
Carbs: 6.6g

Fats: 16.7g
Proteins: 2g

Sodium: 204mg
Sugar: 0.5g

Low-Carb Banoffee Pie

Serves: 12
Prep Time: 40 mins
Keep everyone happy with this satisfying and Ketogenic masterpiece dessert.

Ingredients
- 1 cup organic almond flour
- 1 cup Stevia
- 6 tablespoons organic butter
- 2 cups + 2 tablespoons organic heavy cream
- 1 tablespoon banana flavor

Directions
1. Preheat the oven to 300 degrees F and grease a 9-inch pie pan.
2. Melt the butter over low heat and add almond flour and 1/3 cup stevia.
3. Press the dough firmly into a pan and transfer in the oven.
4. Bake the crust for about 20 minutes and keep aside.
5. Put ¾ cup + 2 tablespoons of the heavy cream and 2/3 cup Stevia in a saucepan and stir well.
6. Boil this mixture on a medium heat stirring constantly until the mixture thickens.
7. Remove the pan from heat and add banana flavor.
8. Allow to cool in the fridge and spread the toffee on the crust.
9. Top with the remaining whipped cream and serve chilled.

Nutrition
Calories: 323
Carbs: 11.5g
Fats: 27.8g
Proteins: 3.3g
Sodium: 70mg
Sugar: 0g

Brownie Truffle Pie

Serves: 10
Prep Time: 55 mins
This is a decadent low carb brownie truffle pie recipe with a press-in almond flour crust and a gooey brownie filling.

Ingredients
Crust:
- 3 tablespoons coconut flour
- 5 tablespoons butter, cut into small pieces
- 1¼ cups almond flour
- 1 tablespoon granulated Swerve
- ¼ teaspoon salt
- 4 tablespoons ice water

Filling:
- 6 tablespoons cocoa powder
- 1 teaspoon baking powder
- ¼ cup melted butter
- ½ cup almond flour
- 6 tablespoons Swerve Sweetener
- 2 large eggs
- 5 tablespoons water
- 1 tablespoon Sukrin Fiber Syrup
- 3 tablespoons sugar-free chocolate chips
- ½ teaspoon vanilla extract

Topping:
- 2 tablespoons Swerve Sweetener
- ½ ounce sugar-free dark chocolate
- 1 cup whipping cream
- ¼ teaspoon vanilla extract

Directions
1. **Crust:** Preheat the oven to 325 degrees F and grease a pie pan.
2. Mix together almond flour, coconut flour, water, Swerve, butter, and salt in a bowl to form a dough.
3. Press evenly into the pie pan and transfer in the oven.
4. Bake for about 12 minutes and remove from the oven.

5. **Filling:** Whisk together the cocoa powder, almond flour, Swerve, and baking powder in a bowl.
6. Add water, eggs, butter, chocolate chips, and vanilla extract until well combined.
7. Pour this batter into the pie crust and transfer in the oven.
8. Bake for about 30 minutes and allow to cool.
9. **Topping:** Mix together cream, vanilla extract, and Swerve in a large bowl.
10. Beat until stiff peaks form and layer over cooled filling.
11. Top with dark chocolate and chill until completely set.

Nutrition
Calories: 374
Carbs: 5.7g
Fats: 33.9g
Proteins: 8.5g
Sodium: 280mg
Sugar: 0.8g

• Low Carb Grasshopper Pie

Serves: 8
Prep Time: 25 mins
This is a perfect breakfast recipe to brighten your day!

Ingredients
- ½ cup cocoa powder
- ½ teaspoon baking powder
- ¼ cup coconut oil
- 2 tablespoons chocolate syrup
- 2 cups ground flax seeds
- 3 teaspoons Stevia powder
- Pinch of salt
- ½ cup smooth almond butter
- 2 eggs
- Mint ice cream, sugar-free

Directions
1. Preheat the oven to 350 degrees F and grease a large pie dish.
2. Mix together all dry ingredients in a bowl and keep aside.
3. Mix almond butter, eggs, chocolate syrup and coconut oil in another bowl.
4. Combine the two mixtures to form a crumbly dough and press in the pie dish.
5. Transfer in the oven and bake for about 12 minutes.
6. Allow to cool and fill with sugar-free mint ice cream to serve.

Nutrition
Calories: 358
Carbs: 15.2g
Fats: 26.5g
Proteins: 11g
Sodium: 51mg
Sugar: 4.3g

Chapter 13: Delicious Pizza Recipes

• Keto Breakfast Pizza

Serves: 6
Prep Time: 30 mins
Keto Breakfast Pizza is super easy to make with all the great flavor of eggs.

Ingredients
- 2 tablespoons coconut flour
- 2 cups cauliflower, grated
- ½ teaspoon salt
- 1 tablespoon psyllium husk powder
- 4 eggs

Toppings:
- Avocado
- Smoked Salmon
- Herbs
- Olive oil
- Spinach

Directions
1. Preheat the oven to 360 degrees and grease a pizza tray.
2. Mix together all ingredients in a bowl, except toppings, and keep aside.
3. Pour the pizza dough onto the pan and mold it into an even pizza crust using hands.
4. Top the pizza with toppings and transfer in the oven.
5. Bake for about 15 minutes until golden brown and remove from the oven to serve.

Nutrition
Calories: 454   Fats: 31g   Sodium: 1325mg
Carbs: 16g   Proteins: 22g   Sugar: 4.4g

• Coconut Flour Pizza

Serves: 4
Prep Time: 35 mins
Coconut Flour Pizza Crust is so easy to prepare and delicious to eat. You can make a thin crispy crust or a thick crust from this mixture.

Ingredients
- 2 tablespoons psyllium husk powder
- ¾ cup coconut flour
- 1 teaspoon garlic powder
- ½ teaspoon salt
- ½ teaspoon baking soda
- 1 cup boiling water
- 1 teaspoon apple cider vinegar
- 3 eggs

Toppings
- 3 tablespoons tomato sauce
- 1½ oz. Mozzarella cheese
- 1 tablespoon basil, freshly chopped

Directions
1. Preheat the oven to 350 degrees F and grease a baking sheet.
2. Mix coconut flour, salt, psyllium husk powder, and garlic powder until fully combined.
3. Add eggs, apple cider vinegar, and baking soda and knead with boiling water.
4. Place the dough out on a baking sheet and top with the toppings.
5. Transfer in the oven and bake for about 20 minutes.
6. Dish out and serve warm.

Nutrition
Calories: 173
Carbs: 16.8g

Fats: 7.4g
Proteins: 10.4g

Sodium: 622mg
Sugar: 0.9g

Mini Pizza Crusts

Serves: 4
Prep Time: 20 mins
These mini pizza crusts are an easy, delicious and low carb substitutes to traditional pizzas!

Ingredients
- 1 cup coconut flour, sifted
- 8 large eggs, 5 whole eggs and 3 egg whites
- ½ teaspoon baking powder
- Italian spices, to taste
- Salt and black pepper, to taste

For the pizza sauce
- 2 garlic cloves, crushed
- 1 teaspoon dried basil
- ½ cup tomato sauce
- ¼ teaspoon sea salt

Directions
1. Preheat the oven to 350 degrees F and grease a baking tray.
2. Whisk together eggs and egg whites in a large bowl and stir in the coconut flour, baking powder, Italian spices, salt, and black pepper.
3. Make small dough balls from this mixture and press on the baking tray.
4. Transfer in the oven and bake for about 20 minutes.
5. Allow pizza bases to cool and keep aside.
6. Combine all ingredients for the pizza sauce together and sit at room temperature for half an hour.
7. Spread this pizza sauce over the pizza crusts and serve.

Nutrition
Calories: 170
Fats: 10.5g
Sodium: 461mg
Carbs: 5.7g
Proteins: 13.6g
Sugar: 2.3g

Keto Pepperoni Pizza

Serves: 4
Prep Time: 40 mins
This pizza has everything that you want, like the deliciousness of pepperoni, tomato-sauce, and cheese.

Ingredients
Crust
- 6 oz. mozzarella cheese, shredded
- 4 eggs

Topping
- 1 teaspoon dried oregano
- 1½ oz. pepperoni
- 3 tablespoons tomato paste
- 5 oz. mozzarella cheese, shredded
- Olives

Directions
1. Preheat the oven to 400 degrees F and grease a baking sheet.
2. Whisk together eggs and cheese in a bowl and spread on a baking sheet.
3. Transfer in the oven and bake for about 15 minutes until golden.
4. Remove from the oven and allow it to cool.
5. Increase the oven temperature to 450 degrees F.
6. Spread the tomato paste on the crust and top with oregano, pepperoni, cheese, and olives on top.
7. Bake for another 10 minutes and serve hot.

Nutrition
Calories: 356
Carbs: 6.1g
Fats: 23.8g
Proteins: 30.6g
Sodium: 790mg
Sugar: 1.8g

Thin Crust Low Carb Pizza

Serves: 6
Prep Time: 25 mins
This is a quick, easy, and delicious recipe for thin-crust and low carb pizza.

Ingredients
- 2 tablespoons tomato sauce
- 1/8 teaspoon black pepper
- 1/8 teaspoon chili flakes
- 1 piece low-carb pita bread
- 2 ounces low-moisture mozzarella cheese
- 1/8 teaspoon garlic powder

Toppings:
- Bacon, roasted red peppers, spinach, olives, pesto, artichokes, salami, pepperoni, roast beef, prosciutto, avocado, ham, chili paste, Sriracha

Directions
1. Preheat the oven to 450 degrees F and grease a baking dish.
2. Mix together tomato sauce, black pepper, chili flakes, and garlic powder in a bowl and keep aside.
3. Place the low-carb pita bread in the oven and bake for about 2 minutes.
4. Remove from oven and spread the tomato sauce on it.
5. Add mozzarella cheese and top with your favorite toppings.
6. Bake again for 3 minutes and dish out.

Nutrition
Calories: 254
Carbs: 12.9g
Fats: 16g
Proteins: 19.3g
Sodium: 255mg
Sugar: 2.8g

• BBQ Chicken Pizza

Serves: 4
Prep Time: 30 mins
This is similar to a recipe I had at a popular pizza place. My family loves it!

Ingredients
Dairy Free Pizza Crust
- 6 tablespoons Parmesan cheese
- 6 large eggs
- 3 tablespoons psyllium husk powder
- Salt and black pepper, to taste
- 1½ teaspoons Italian seasoning

Toppings
- 6 oz. rotisserie chicken, shredded
- 4 oz. cheddar cheese
- 1 tablespoon mayonnaise
- 4 tablespoons tomato sauce
- 4 tablespoons BBQ sauce

Directions
1. Preheat the oven to 400 degrees F and grease a baking dish.
2. Place all Pizza Crust ingredients in an immersion blender and blend until smooth.
3. Spread dough mixture onto the baking dish and transfer in the oven.
4. Bake for about 10 minutes and top with favorite toppings.
5. Bake for about 3 minutes and dish out.

Nutrition
Calories: 356
Carbs: 2.9g
Fats: 24.5g
Proteins: 24.5g
Sodium: 396mg
Sugar: 0.6g

Buffalo Chicken Crust Pizza

Serves: 6
Prep Time: 25 mins
This pizza has a little kick of buffalo wing flavor. Have your pizza and wings together!

Ingredients
- 1 cup whole milk mozzarella, shredded
- 1 teaspoon dried oregano
- 2 tablespoons butter
- 1 pound chicken thighs, boneless and skinless
- 1 large egg
- ¼ teaspoon black pepper
- ¼ teaspoon salt
- 1 stalk celery
- 3 tablespoons Franks Red Hot Original
- 1 stalk green onion
- 1 tablespoon sour cream
- 1 ounce bleu cheese, crumbled

Directions
1. Preheat the oven to 400 degrees F and grease a baking dish.
2. Process chicken thighs in a food processor until smooth.
3. Transfer to a large bowl and add egg, ½ cup of shredded mozzarella, oregano, black pepper, and salt to form a dough.
4. Spread the chicken dough in the baking dish and transfer in the oven
5. Bake for about 25 minutes and keep aside.
6. Meanwhile, heat butter and add celery, and cook for about 4 minutes.
7. Mix Franks Red Hot Original with the sour cream in a small bowl.
8. Spread the sauce mixture over the crust, layer with the cooked celery and remaining ½ cup of mozzarella and the bleu cheese.
9. Bake for another 10 minutes, until the cheese is melted

Nutrition
Calories: 172

Fats: 12.9g

Sodium: 172mg

Carbs: 1g

Proteins: 13.8g

Sugar: 0.2g

• Fresh Bell Pepper Basil Pizza

Serves: 3
Prep Time: 25 mins
Flavorful fresh bell pepper and basil make this pizza unique and delicious.

Ingredients
Pizza Base
- ½ cup almond flour
- 2 tablespoons cream cheese
- 1 teaspoon Italian seasoning
- ½ teaspoon black pepper
- 6 ounces mozzarella cheese
- 2 tablespoons psyllium husk
- 2 tablespoons fresh Parmesan cheese
- 1 large egg
- ½ teaspoon salt

Toppings
- 4 ounces cheddar cheese, shredded
- ¼ cup Marinara sauce
- 2/3 medium bell pepper
- 1 medium vine tomato
- 3 tablespoons basil, fresh chopped

Directions
1. Preheat the oven to 400 degrees F and grease a baking dish.
2. Microwave mozzarella cheese for about 30 seconds and top with the remaining pizza crust.
3. Add the remaining pizza ingredients to the cheese and mix together.
4. Flatten the dough and transfer in the oven.
5. Bake for about 10 minutes and remove pizza from the oven.
6. Top the pizza with the toppings and bake for another 10 minutes.
7. Remove pizza from the oven and allow to cool.

Nutrition
Calories: 411	Fats: 31.3g	Sodium: 152mg
Carbs: 6.4g	Proteins: 22.2g	Sugar: 2.8g

Keto Thai Chicken Flatbread Pizza

Serves: 12
Prep Time: 25 mins
Skip the same-old pizza and try our Thai chicken flatbread pizza instead.

Ingredients
Peanut Sauce
- 2 tablespoons rice wine vinegar
- 4 tablespoons reduced sugar ketchup
- 4 tablespoons pbfit
- 4 tablespoons soy sauce
- 4 tablespoons coconut oil
- ½ lime, juiced
- 1 teaspoon fish sauce

Pizza Base
- ¾ cup almond flour
- 3 tablespoons cream cheese
- ½ teaspoon garlic powder
- 8 oz. mozzarella cheese
- 1 tablespoon psyllium husk powder
- 1 large egg
- ½ teaspoon onion powder
- ½ teaspoon ginger
- ½ teaspoon black pepper
- ½ teaspoon salt

Toppings
- 3 oz. mung bean sprouts
- 2 medium green onions
- 2 tablespoons peanuts
- 2 chicken thighs
- 6 oz. mozzarella cheese
- 1½ oz. carrots, shredded

Directions
1. Preheat oven to 400 degrees F and grease a baking tray.
2. Mix together all peanut sauce ingredients and set aside.
3. Microwave cream cheese and mozzarella cheese for the pizza base for 1 minute.
4. Add eggs, then mix together with all dry ingredients.
5. Arrange dough onto a baking tray and bake for about 15 minutes.
6. Flip pizza and top with sauce, chopped chicken, shredded carrots, and mozzarella.
7. Bake again for 10 minutes, or until cheese has melted.
8. Top with bean sprouts, spring onion, peanuts, and cilantro.

Nutrition
Calories: 268
Carbs: 3.2g
Fats: 21g
Proteins: 15g
Sodium: 94mg
Sugar: 0.2g

Apple and Ham Flatbread Pizza

Serves: 8
Prep Time: 15 mins
Topped with onions, ham, apples, cheese and thyme, it is sure to be a hit with the entire family.

Ingredients
For the crust:
- ¾ cup almond flour
- ½ teaspoon sea salt
- 2 cups mozzarella cheese, shredded
- 2 tablespoons cream cheese
- 1/8 teaspoon dried thyme

For the topping:
- ½ small red onion, cut into thin slices
- 4 ounces low carbohydrate ham, cut into chunks
- Salt and black pepper, to taste
- 1 cup Mexican blend cheese, grated
- ¼ medium apple, sliced
- 1/8 teaspoon dried thyme

Directions
1. Preheat the oven to 425 degrees F and grease a 12-inch pizza pan.
2. Boil water and steam cream cheese, mozzarella cheese, almond flour, thyme, and salt.
3. When the cheese melts enough, knead for a few minutes to thoroughly mix dough.
4. Make a ball out of the dough and arrange in the pizza pan.
5. Poke holes all over the dough with a fork and transfer in the oven.
6. Bake for about 8 minutes until golden brown and reset the oven setting to 350 degrees F.
7. Sprinkle ¼ cup of the Mexican blend cheese over the flatbread and top with onions, apples, and ham.
8. Cover with the remaining ¾ cup of the Mexican blend cheese and sprinkle with the thyme, salt, and black pepper.
9. Bake for about 7 minutes until cheese is melted and crust is golden brown.
10. Remove the flatbread from the oven and allow to cool before cutting.
11. Slice into desired pieces and serve.

Nutrition
Calories: 179

Fats: 13.6g

Sodium: 539mg

Carbs: 5.3g

Proteins: 10.4g

Sugar: 2.1g

55326379R00053

Made in the USA
Middletown, DE
16 July 2019